# The Librarian's Quick Guide to Internet Resources

## Second Edition

Jenny Lynne Semenza

Upstart Books

## Acknowledgments

This book is dedicated to my husband Nick and his ability to get me Internet access anywhere, anytime. Special thanks go to my daughter Shanna for her support and assistance. I would like to thank the professional, understanding, and wonderful staff at Upstart Books, particularly Virginia Harrison. I am also grateful to Arlene, Kay, Nanette, Kristin, Cheryl, Nola, and everyone else who has sent me great websites.

Published by Highsmith Press LLC
W5527 Highway 106
P.O. Box 800
Fort Atkinson, Wisconsin 53538-0800
1-800-558-2110

© Jenny Semenza, 2001
Cover by Alison Relyea

The paper used in this publication meets the minimum requirements of American National Standard for Information Science — Permanence of Paper for Printed Library Material. ANSI/NISO Z39.48-1992.

# Contents

# Introduction

As is necessary with all things Internet, this second edition has been completely revised. In section one, the information on e-mail has been substantially increased to include topics such as hoaxes and viruses. A new section entitled "Finding Information on the Web" has been added and includes more information on search engines and search strategies. In section two, many new websites and categories have been added and all entries have been verified for accuracy.

This handbook for both novice and expert Internet users has been created to help librarians find useful, relevant information while developing a better understanding of how to search and share the many rich resources on the Web. The information chosen for the *Quick Guide* evolved out of the workshops I teach to both school and public librarians and out of my work as a reference librarian. In selecting the over 600 websites included here (of which approximately 300 are new in this edition), emphasis was placed on those that will be of practical value in serving students, teachers and the general, broad interests of public library patrons.

In the first few pages of this book you'll find a quick overview of the Internet, including e-mail, mailing lists, newsgroups, the World Wide Web, FTP, telnet and search engines. It also has instructions on how to use Netscape Navigator and Microsoft Internet Explorer for browsing the Web. I've included this brief review of the most basic terminology and functions to assist your use and understanding the Internet, but the real focus of this handbook is on the websites located in Part 2.

## What's Included, What's Not ...

I have included many sites that I use on a regular basis to help everyone from fourth graders to senior citizens at the reference desk. I have tried to select sites for their accuracy, stability and usability. This does not mean that these sites won't move, become inaccurate or unusable. In fact, change is the one thing we can be certain of. On the whole, however, these sites will be easier to use and will be more likely to announce changes in addresses or site focus than some of the more ephemeral locations I passed up in my selection process. I have included a few sites that have been evolving. They have started with a few good items and have continued to grow and become better.

The certainty of change in websites is a good caution to share with reference patrons you serve. I try to remind them that the content on web pages is constantly changing. This makes collecting the information you need right away important because the reference may be gone when you return to recheck it later.

Point of view or bias is also a good issue to keep in mind. Sites are put up every day by individuals and by companies trying to sell something and by self-interest groups who may not be looking for a profit, but are definitely trying to sell their message.

## Authority

I have used the term "authority" throughout this guide. Originally, I had hoped that the sites I would include would actually state who was responsible for the intellectual content. Unfortunately, sites rarely have that information. For the purposes of this book, "authority" means the person or institution ultimately responsible for the page. In many cases, the person or institution that is responsible is not the person who wrote the content. There were a few instances when no responsible party was listed for any part of the site, but the quality of the information made it worth inclusion.

## Additional Sources

Of course, I could not index the entire Web. Nor could I necessarily find every useful or relevant reference website. So, I have included a list of other online reference sites (on page 78) to help you find other resources.

Although my primary goal was to find library reference sites, not curriculum or teacher resources, I have included a number of pointers to help educators find some great subject-related activities, lesson plans and links. In addition to subject headings for curriculum areas, I have also included a section called "Education: Teacher Student Resource" (page 40). The resources here are complex indexes to education sites on the World Wide Web. Sites that offer lesson plans are indicated with a crayon symbol  ✎ . If there is a grade level assigned or intended, this has been included in the site description.

Many of the websites chosen for the *Guide* were selected because they make great jumping off points to their topic or subject area. Those that are especially rich have been indicated with a link symbol ∞.

Some final caveats include: Please assume that everything you see on the Web is copyrighted unless it states otherwise. Most clip-art and public domain materials are the exceptions. When in doubt, read the help screens. Help screens, "about the site" material and FAQs are invaluable when trying to efficiently use or understand a site.

I am hopeful you will find many, many interesting and new ideas and resources for your patrons.

# Part 1

# A Basic Guide to Internet Tools and Procedures

While the focus of *The Librarian's Quick Guide* is on the rich resources contained in the websites listed in the next section, the Internet is really much more than just websites. It is a method of communication, information dispersal and networking. E-mail, mailing lists and newsgroups facilitate communication with friends, colleagues and other individuals. The World Wide Web, FTP and telnet are ways of acquiring and disseminating knowledge, opinions, data, resources, points of view and information. Search engines, plug-ins and browsers all enhance and extend the possibilities of the Web. In this section, I've included brief descriptions, definitions and "how-tos" on some of the ways these parts work together to create a stimulating source for you and your patrons.

## Getting Connected

In the most simple terms, the Internet is a system of phone, fiber optic, satellite, cable or other communication lines which connect computers that are always on, called "servers." Any server anywhere in the world can talk to any other server over the telecommunications infrastructure. In order to be part of the Internet you can either have a server or rent space on someone else's.

AOL, AT&T, MCI and other communications companies have servers in multiple locations and rent out space on their servers to individuals. While the size of these companies is noteworthy, no single company is the Internet. Smaller Internet Service Providers (ISPs) are everywhere: look in the phone book under "Internet." A good ISP will usually help new customers configure their computers and load software, give classes on how to use software and make other help available. Once you have an Internet account with an ISP, you will have access to electronic mail (also known as e-mail), Usenet (also known as newsgroups), telnet, File Transfer Protocol (FTP) and the World Wide Web (WWW).

### Electronic mail: E-mail

The sending of electronic correspondence or e-mail is just one activity that is available on the Internet. In order to access your server space you will be assigned a word to use as a "log-on" or "log-in" name or user identification. This log-on name is usually your name or some variation thereof. Logging on is the process of making your computer communicate with the server computer.

E-mail is semi-private in that it is sent to whomever you choose to send it to, but occasionally it can go astray and wind up in the wrong mailbox. It can get lost in cyberspace if you have addressed it incorrectly or misplaced a dot or "tilde." It can get bounced if the recipient has changed accounts, has an account that is too full, or if the recipient's system is down. In any of these cases, people such as system administrators who try and return lost mail will see your e-mail. E-mail is not publicly archived anywhere on the Internet, but some institutions do keep track of e-mail and others make tape backups of their systems, including e-mail accounts, and track Internet usage in general. Many workplaces have a non-privacy policy regarding the accounts they provide for employees. They may also have "acceptable use" statements about how e-mail and the Internet should be used.

Do not send passwords, credit card numbers or other private information through e-mail unless you can be certain it is a secure transmission. If you do need to send sensitive information via e-mail, use a software program that enables the encryption of the data. This requires that both you and the person on the receiving end have the encryption key to encrypt and decrypt the message. You can find more information about this topic at: Introduction of PGP http://web.bham.ac.uk/N.M.Queen/pgp/pgp.html.

**Hoaxes, Myths and Urban Legends:** Stories of all kinds flood the Internet like an overfull river, but instead of just coming through once, the stories come and go and come back like the ocean tide. Be aware that most stories on the Internet are not true. They sound like they're true, sometimes they even quote real sounding sources. But most of the tales sent around are false. And many of them have been around the 'net a few times. There are some great web pages (see p. 57) to help you figure out which of the stories are patently false.

**Spam:** Spam is defined at dictionary.com as: "Unsolicited e-mail, often of a commercial nature, sent indiscriminately to multiple mailing lists, individuals or newsgroups. If you have an e-mail account, sooner or later you will receive spam.

**Netiquette:** There are a few conventions to be aware of when communicating through e-mail. One of them is that using ALLCAPS is the equivalent of shouting. Another convention is the use of emoticons such as smileys. :) or :-) are the most common smileys. If you tilt your head to the left you will see that both of those sets of symbols look like smiling faces lying on their sides. There are many web pages you can use for decoding the emoticons, Internet acronyms and etiquette (see p. 44).

**Viruses:** Unfortunately viruses can be spread by e-mail. This is usually accomplished when the e-mail recipient opens an attachment. The best defense against viruses is to not open attachments unless you know what it is supposed to be and who it is from. Also, buy, install and regularly update a good anti-virus program like McCaffee or Norton. Viruses are created every day so regular updates are necessary. See your software literature for instructions.

## Mailing lists

Mailing lists are forums you can join by e-mail to discuss all kinds of topics—thousands, in fact. Some are private, which means that they have a specific number of members and do not take new ones. Some are public, which means that they allow anyone to sign up and be part of the list. Members of a mailing list send an e-mail to the list address. The e-mail is then automatically distributed to every other member's e-mail address.

Some lists are moderated, meaning all e-mail goes to one or several people serving as moderators first and they approve the e-mail or reject it according to established criteria. If the e-mail is approved, it gets sent to the rest of the list. If it gets rejected, it usually gets returned to the author with an explanation.

Mailing lists are sometimes called lists, Listservs™ or Majordomo lists. Majordomo and Listserv are the names of software programs that automate the list process.

A mailing list titled School Library Media & Network Communications will also have an acronym (LM_NET) which serves as the username in the e-mail address. The list address looks like this: LM_NET@listserv.syr.edu. To subscribe to a mailing list, you must send an e-mail to the automated process or the owner of the list. In this example the address would be listserv@listserv.syr.edu. The form of the subscribe statement or joining request is: "subscribe LM_NET yourfirstname yourlastname." Put the subscribe statement in the body of the e-mail and leave the subject line blank. Most mailing lists follow this pattern for subscription requests.

Once you have joined a list, you will receive an official welcome message with the directions for getting off the list, a review of who is on the list and a short statement of topic. Save this message, or print it and file it, because you will want to get off the list eventually, whether for a vacation or because it is irrelevant to your current interests. The welcome notice should tell you if all messages are being retained in an online archives and what the e-mail rules or accepted netiquette guidelines are for the list. (See p. 63.)

## Newsgroups

Newsgroups, are often referred to as Usenet or Net news. Newsgroups are similar to bulletin boards in that they do not require a membership or subscription and are similar to mailing lists in that they are restricted to a specific subject. Some news forums are moderated. Access to newsgroups are available from Netscape via Messenger and from Microsoft via Outlook or there are programs you can use to access Newsgroups. Your ISP should be able to recommend one to you. Newsgroups are considered a public forum and the messages on them are archived on the Internet.

Newsgroups are arranged into broad subject categories. The most popular are alt., comp., k12., misc., news., rec., sci., soc. and talk. The goal of a newsgroup address is to state the newsgroup's subject focus. Most addresses consist of three to five words and abbreviations strung together with periods in between. For example *comp.internet.library* and *comp.internet.net-happenings* are both members of the large computer category and both discuss Internet issues. It is only at the third abbreviation or word that they differ. The first, *comp.internet.libraries* discusses libraries and the Internet. The second, *comp.internet.net-happenings* announces new websites on the Internet.

Newsgroups often collect the answers to questions that are asked frequently, into FAQs or "Frequently Asked Questions." FAQs have considerable information about the topic of the group. For example, the diabetes group (misc.health.diabetes) has produced an FAQ which covers subjects from diet to blood sugar testing apparatus. Mailing lists and some websites also produce FAQs. (See p. 68.)

## Chat and Instant Messenger

A popular feature of the Internet, Chat or Instant Messenger, allows instant communication in real time. In other words you type a sentence and the sentence shows up on the screens of anyone in the "chat room." Someone else can type a sentence, word or smiley face and it will show up immediately on your screen. It is like a phone call except that you are typing. Chat rooms can be public and open to anyone or private between two or more people. Instant Messenger is similar to Chat. There are many different Chat and Instant Messenger programs. You will need to read the help screens to see how they work. See page 32 for sites that are useful when searching for information about a newsgroup, reading the Usenet archive or in finding a group to read.

# World Wide Web

## Basic structure and addresses

When people talk about the Internet they are usually referring to the World Wide Web. The WWW, sometimes referred to as just "the Web," is made up of interconnected collections of information which are known as pages. The pages have been created by individuals, organizations and companies and placed on servers. Web pages are interconnected through the use of hypertext links. "Hypertext markup language" or HTML is the coding that make the web pages link to each other and display properly. A link can be either text or images that are clicked on to go to another page. The "Home" page is usually the top level page or table of contents page of a site on the Web. "Website" refers to all of the pages put up by a single organization or individual and "web page" is any single web document.

All web pages have addresses referred to as "URLs." URL stands for Uniform Resource Locator. The address contains the designation for the server computer, the directory and the file. For example:

http://www.nasa.gov/hqpao/welcome.html

is the URL for a web page which is part of the overall NASA website. Breaking down the address or URL further and reading it from left to right, you can discover information about the website.

The first part of the address up to the two slashes tells the browser software what kind of Internet source or protocol it is viewing. While it is no longer necessary to type http:// into most browsers, the underlying concept remains important. There are other protocols in existence such as FTP and there could be new protocols in the future.

1. **http://** tells the program to interpret the document as a web page.
2. **www.** is the name the ISP has given the server computer.
3. **nasa.** is the name of the organization or some other ISP identifying word.
4. **gov.** is the domain designation for a federal

government site.

Slashes are the punctuation marks of a URL. The slash after .gov indicates the end of the server designation part of the address. We can tell that hqpao/ is a directory because it has slashes on both sides and does not end in an extension such as .html or .shtml. Sites can have multiple directories to better organize their files. This directory contains the document *welcome.html.*

There are seven standard domain designations used in the United States. These two-to-three-letter codes are .com for commercial "for profit" businesses, .net for network sites, .org for "non profit" organizations, .mil for the military, .gov for the government, .edu for educational institutions and .us for United States. The .us is used for government sites. The United States is unique in having so many different domains. Internationally, servers use the country code as the last domain code (i.e. .au for Australia and .ca for Canada).

With the explosion of sites on the Web, there has been a change in the usage of the domains. .net, .com and .org can all be used for whatever reason a person likes. Recently .biz and .info have been approved for use commercially. See the Internet Corporation for Assigned Names and Numbers (ICANN) at http://www.icann.com/ for more information.

Another example is:

http://www.isu.edu/library/reference/ready.htm

- **http://** The protocol
- **www.isu.edu/** The name of the server.institution.domain
- **library/** The name of a directory on the server
- **reference/** The name of a directory in the library directory
- **ready.htm** The name of a file in the reference directory in the library directory on the www.isu.edu server

## Troubleshooting faulty URLs

If you get a "Document Not Found" message, you can backspace to any slash to back your way up the directory tree of the site. For example, if <http://www.nasa.gov/hqpao/welcome.html> did not work, you could backspace over the welcome.html. If a table of contents or default page did not come up with this change, backspace over the hqpao/ to find the main page for the site. When a page is renamed, the address for it becomes inaccurate. By backspacing to the nearest slash, you can often locate the document you were seeking.

Another type of address includes a ~ (tilde). The

tilde indicates personal or individual Web pages. For example: http://www.isu.edu/~semejenn/ is one of my personal Web pages. You can tell from the server designation that I am at ISU or Idaho State University. The tilde means that I am associated with the university and have an account on this server. It also means the contents on the page may reside on the university server, but the university is not responsible for nor does it necessarily approve of the contents. It also indicates that the site is transitory. If I were to end my association with the university, the site would be deleted.

In order to access the Web, you must have an account with an ISP and have software loaded on your machine. The software is generically called a "web browser." There are many brands of web browsers including Lynx, Opera and Mosaic. The most popular browsers are Microsoft's Internet Explorer and Netscape's Navigator.

The World Wide Web now hosts all kinds of media. Pictures, images, sound, movies, real time chat, interactive applications and databases are just a few of the features. The best way to understand the Web and get familiar with it is to use it. I recommend searching for something that interests you. The Web contains a wealth of information including home repair, science, movies, fiction, shopping centers, landscaping, travel, crafts, arts, medical information and news/weather. In the search process, you will begin to understand the complexity as well as the possibilities of the Internet. Unfortunately, the Web provides a forum for a host of misinformation, so be aware that you must carefully evaluate what you find.

### File Transfer Protocol: FTP

This function is now bundled with many web browsers. It can transfer a file from a server anywhere in the world to your computer's hard drive. FTP is the mechanism for downloading software from the Internet. FTP links can be embedded in web pages. If you need assistance using FTP contact your ISP or help desk.

### Telnet

Telnet links are embedded in web documents. When the link is clicked on, it opens a screen or window in front of the normal browser frame. This telnet window acts as if it were directly connected to the mainframe or computer system on the other server. Many library catalogs are still mainframe-based and command-driven, so to access them, a telnet session must be used. If the library system requires a log-on and password, the telnet session will require a log-on and password. Some web browsers need to be configured to automatically launch telnet when a telnet address is

clicked on. Talk to your computer help desk or your ISP to get instructions on how to do this.

# Finding Information on the Web: Search Engines

Many search engines and directories are available on the Internet for searching the World Wide Web. None of these search engines index the entire Web, in part because the Web is growing and changing rapidly and in part because of the size of the Web. A search engine does not execute a search by going out onto the Web to look for sites when you type in a request, instead, it goes through an index that resides on its own server. Each search engine on the Internet has a unique index of sites, some of which overlap. Most search engines now offer the ability for individuals to register a website with the search engine so it will be included in the index. As every search engine will produce unique results, use more than one to ensure more complete search results.

## Search Result Retrieval

When web pages are added to the search engine database, several main content areas on the page are indexed. These content areas include the title tag, the meta tags, the first 100 or so words and the major headings. Meta tags are HTML codes that do not appear in the normal viewing of a web page. Two commonly used meta-tags are "description," which is a summary of the site and "keywords," which list related terms or synonyms. Meta-tags are frequently weighted higher than the text of a document. When you execute a search the search engine uses a complex mathematical algorithm to determine the ranking of the web pages. Each search engine has a unique algorithm that it uses to rank the search results from most relevant to least.

Most of the time a combination of the "content areas" are used to rank web pages. However, some search engines allow companies to purchase their rankings. For instance Pepsi can purchase the right to be retrieved first whenever the word "Pepsi" is searched. At this time only Go.com uses paid rankings. Another trick is to use popularity for ranking web pages. Popularity is determined by the number of times a web page has been clicked on when a similar search has been executed. Still another method of ranking is by "freshness." The sites where content has changed most recently are ranked higher. All of these maneuvers are used in order to bring back the most relevant results to the searcher.

# Types of Search Engines

## Directory search engines

A directory search engine is characterized by a hierarchical subject arrangement. The contents of the index can be searched by clicking down through the subject hierarchy or by using the search box. Yahoo! is probably the best known of the Directory Search Engines. Humans instead of computer programs create the indexes, either by searching the Web for appropriate sites or by wading through the hundreds of URLs that get submitted for indexing. This method of index creation has several implications. First, sites are organized in categories where similar pages can be found together. Second, there is less garbage in the results because humans have pre-filtered the index, disallowing garbage sites. Third, links can get out of date because humans also have to remove the dead links. Fourth, the directory's index is small because humans cannot compile addresses as quickly as computers. Most directory search engines are now affiliated with one of the larger standard search engines. For instance, Yahoo! will retrieve results from Google when it cannot find sites within its own index. Directory search engines are useful for finding one good site on almost any topic and finding information on important or distinctive people, places and things. I have used it to find tax return forms for other states and information about cities and states such as restaurants, real estate agents and businesses. (See p. 80.)

## Standard search engines

Standard search engines are characterized by huge databases indexing millions of web pages. The pages are found and indexed by computer programs called harvesters, robots, bots and spiders. Many standard search engines have made agreements with directories such as Yahoo! and provide the directory information on the first page. Clicking through the subject hierarchies access the directory and human-created index. Use the search box to access the enormous standard search engine's database.

Many standard search engines use the same database. For instance, "Inktomi" is the name of a very large database of web pages, but it is not a search engine. There is no site called Inktomi that you can use to search for web pages. Instead, Inktomi sells its database information to search engines such as MSN Search, AOL Search and GoTo.com (current as of 7/5/2001). Even though they all access the Inktomi database, the retrieved results can be very different because the search algorithm is unique to the search engine, not the underlying database.

In general, standard search engines are the best place to start when searching for most topics. Use one or more if the topic is obscure such as a medical condition or very specialized like the native plants of North Dakota. They are also useful when looking for a lot of information on a single subject. Standard Search Engines are known to retrieve hundreds if not millions of potentially relevant sites. (See p. 82.)

## Meta search engines

This type of search engine accesses multiple search engines and executes a search on them simultaneously. Meta search engines can only do simplistic keyword searches. Use them to get an overview of what is available on the Web on a specific topic. They are also useful when you are not finding anything via other search methods, because they access so many different and unique databases. (See p. 81.)

## Specialized search engines

Specialized search engines are format or subject specific. These do not attempt to index the entire Web, but focus on one section or topic. There are literally thousands of these types of search engines on the Web. They include Liszt which searches for mailing lists, Ditto which searches for pictures and WebRing which searches for web rings. Web rings are like clubs that link together a bunch of sites on a similar topic. Specialized search engines can make finding everything on a topic much easier. One of the continuing problems with the Net and search engines is that the number of web pages is growing faster than the search engines can index. Not one search engine indexes the entire Web. At most, 70% of the Web is indexed by any one search engine. These subject or format specific search engines become invaluable at finding the remaining 30% of the Web. (See p. 81.)

## Search engines for kids

There are lots of search engines on the Web that have been designed to help kids of all ages find information. There are several goals at work in these engines. The first is to provide a solid collection of web pages of relevant information. Second is to create an environment that is kid friendly. This includes an effort to eliminate hate and porn sites from the databases. These search engines include directories, standard search engines and meta search engines. (See p. 80.)

# Search Strategies

There are many search strategies to use including phrase and Boolean searching. Phrase searching requires the use of quotes. If you put Snake River (without quotation marks) into the search box you will, in most cases, get back documents that contain "snake" and "river." As entered, these two words do not have to be next to each other for retrieval of the document. Using quotation marks around "Snake River" makes the search engine search for the words placed next to each other in that exact order.

Some search engines, like Alta Vista, can do case-sensitive searching. "AIDS" is a good example of a search that relies on case sensitivity. If the search engine was not case sensitive, you could get all kinds of hearing aids, riding aids or health aids. Page headings and titles are frequently capitalized. So searching for "Horseback Riding" will find sites that have that phrase as the title or a major heading. If the search word is not capitalized, the search engine will bring back both capitalized and non-capitalized results.

*Boolean searching* is the use of AND, OR or NOT. Boolean-capable search engines require the operators AND, OR or NOT to be in all capital letters. In addition, a + or - can be used to indicate the importance of a word. "Lions AND Tigers NOT 'Beanie Babies'" is a better search than "lions AND tigers." It will require both "Lions" and "Tigers" to be part of the page and exclude all pages that include the phrase "Beanie Babies." It will also require the words "lions" and "tigers" to begin with capital letters. The plus sign requires a word to be present on the document as in "+Lions NOT 'Beanie Babies.'" The word must not be present if the minus sign is used as in "+Lions - 'Beanie Babies.'"

Another code that you can use is a truncation code. Most of the search engines use an asterisk (*) as the truncation code. This code tells the search engine to find all words that begin with the letters preceding the code, for instance "educ*" would find "education," "educational," "educating" and "educated." Be careful when using truncation. If you truncated planning to "plan*" you would get "planning," but you would also retrieve "plans," "plants," "planets" and many more words that begin with "plan."

*Field searching* is the way to target a search to a specific field. Every search engine does this in a different way, so read the help screens. Go to "Advanced Search" on Google and use the boxes to do field searching. Alta Vista requires a specific syntax to do field searching. For instance, to find pages within a specific domain you would type "domain:edu." The search, "+'Citrus Fruit' +domain:edu" would retrieve all web pages that have "citrus fruit" capitalized on the page and reside on an educational institutions server.

Some of the common fields to search are Domain, Title and Link. Domain searching restricts the search results to specific types of servers. For instance a domain search of "Corn" and the .gov domain would bring back web pages that are produced by the government. A Link search finds pages that have a link to the web page address being searched. This is useful when you want to find pages that are similar. So a link search for "sunkist.com "would probably return other fruit related web pages, all of which have a link to the sunkist.com site.

Remember, as no two search engines are alike, the previous search strategies won't work in all of them. I recommend reading the help screens that are provided by these sites to access their databases more efficiently.

# Search Engine Capabilities

| Search Engine | Phrase Search | Boolean Search | Advanced Search? | Case Sensitive? |
|---|---|---|---|---|
| Altavista www.altavista.com | quotes | AND OR NOT +/– | yes | yes |
| Excite excite.com | quotes | AND OR NOT +/– | yes | no |
| Fast Search www.alltheweb.com | quotes | +/– | yes | no |
| Google www.google.com | quotes | +/– | yes | no |
| Hotbot www.hotbot.com | AND OR NOT and phrase searching are available as check boxes/drop down menus. | | yes | no |
| Lycos www.lycos.com | quotes | +/– | yes | no |
| Northern Light www.northernlight.com | quotes | AND OR NOT +/– | no | no |

Every search engine has a default setting. This setting determines what happens when two words are put into the search box. The following table of search engine capabilities was accurate as of 8/29/01. (See also "Search Engines: Standard," page 82.)

# Plug-ins

A plug-in is a software program that is installed on your computer to work with your browser and the Internet. There are plug-ins to view video clips, to listen to audio clips, to enhance a web page's interactivity or to view documents without rendering them into HTML. One of the most common plug-ins for library use is Adobe Acrobat Reader. This reader allows you to view a .pdf (PDF) file. These files are pictures of original documents. The original character and structure of a file is retained because it is not rendered into HTML. Most sites that require plug-ins link to free download sites. (See p. 74.)

# Browsers

Browsers are the programs used to navigate the World Wide Web. They all have several functions in common. One common function is that links are "clickable." As you move the cursor over an active link which is usually highlighted or underlined, the cursor will turn into a hand. This action is very useful when searching for where to click on graphics or image maps. Browsers also have address boxes where you can enter URLs. The two most popular browsers are Netscape Navigator and Microsoft's Internet Explorer. At the top of the web browser window in each of these programs is a row of icons which do the following:

**Home:** This button takes you to a pre-selected page that is called "home." You can choose your home page by changing the preferences or Internet options from the tool bar.

**Back:** Clicking on the back button takes you back to the page previously viewed.

**Forward:** Clicking on the forward button will take you forward a page after you have used the back button.

**Stop:** If a page is taking too long to load or you change your mind about viewing it, click the stop button to make the page stop loading.

**Reload/Refresh:** If a page has not loaded completely, or you believe the content has changed since the last time you viewed it, clicking on this button will send the browser back to the server to retrieve the most current copy of the page.

**Search:** The conveniently located search buttons on the browsers connect to Netscape's and Microsoft's commercially sponsored search pages. These pages do not list all of the search engines that are available, nor do they necessarily list the right one for the topic you wish to search. They do, however, provide instant access to Internet searching.

**History:** The history is a list of all the websites that the web browser has visited. The length of time the history is kept can be set in the Internet options or preferences area of the web browser. This history list can be very useful both for monitoring usage and for finding sites you visited but forgot to write down or bookmark. Microsoft Internet Explorer has a button marked "History" in its icon bar. To access Netscape Navigator's History click on "Communicator" from the drop down menu, then on "Tools" and finally on "History."

## Basic Tasks from the Browser

### Printing a Document
1.  Click on print icon in the tool bar.
    a.  Netscape Navigator click on "OK" or <enter>
    b.  Microsoft Internet Explorer immediately prints the page.

### Printing a Single Page
1.  Click on "File" in the top menu bar, then click on "Print" from the drop down menu. This brings up a dialog box.
2.  Click in the circle by "Pages" under the "Print Range" option of the dialog box.
3.  If you want to print page 12 type "12" in the "From" box and "12" in the "To" box. This will print just page 12.
4.  Click on "OK" or <enter>. There are other print options you can change from this dialog box, including landscape or portrait printing.

### Downloading or Saving a Document
1.  Click on "File" from top menu bar.
2.  Click on "Save as" from the drop down menu. This brings up a dialog box.
3.  Select the drive to which you wish to save the information. This option is located in the top middle of the box called "Save in." Do this by clicking on the triangle pointing down and select the drive and file, by highlighting and clicking.
4.  Select the format type you wish to use. This option is located in the bottom middle of the box called "Save as type." Do this by clicking on the triangle pointing down and select the format.
    a.  HTML format will save the page so it will show

up as a Web page. This includes all of the codes and is useful if you are going to use it/display it on the Web.

   b. Plain Text format will save the page so it will be usable in Word Perfect, Microsoft Word or other word processing programs.

5. Click on "Save" after making selections.

### Saving an Image

1. Move the cursor onto the image you wish to save.
2. Click on the right mouse button.
3. Click on "Save image as" in Netscape Navigator or "Save picture" in Microsoft Internet Explorer. This brings up a dialog box.
4. Select the drive to which you wish to save the information. This option is located in the top middle of the box called "Save in."Do this by clicking on the triangle pointing down and select the drive and file by highlighting and clicking.
5. Click on "Save."

## Bookmarking in the Browser

While surfing the Internet you will frequently come across sites to which you will want to return. A quick way to save the site address is to "bookmark" the page. Bookmarking is an ability that is built into the web browser. In Microsoft's Internet Explorer the bookmark function is called "Favorites." Organize your bookmarks to make them easier to use by adding folders and filing bookmarks into the folders. Create subject folders that make sense for you and give them names that will allow you to find your bookmarks later. For example, I have folders for reference sites, web writing, fun stuff, physics, dance and libraries.

## Bookmarking in Netscape Navigator

### Adding a Bookmark

1. Click on "Bookmarks" icon on the upper part of the browser frame while you are looking at the page you want to save.
2. Click on "Add Bookmark."
3. The next time you click on the "Bookmarks" icon the site name will show in the drop down list.

### Organizing Bookmarks

1. Click on the "Bookmarks" icon on the upper part of the browser frame.
2. Click on "Edit Bookmarks..." which will open up a new window listing all your bookmarks.

### Adding a Folder

1. Highlight the "Bookmarks for" line.
2. Right mouse click to bring up a small dialog box.

3. Left mouse click on "New folder."
4. Name the folder.

*or*

1. Click on "File" from the drop down menu.
2. Then click on "New folder."
3. Name the folder.

   If you highlighted a folder instead of the "Bookmarks for" line you will be creating a subfolder within the other folder. Sometimes this is desirable. I have a folder for Web writing with subfolders for clip-art and html how-to's.

### Moving Bookmarks Into Folders

1. Single click on any bookmark. Hold the left mouse button down and drag the bookmark to the destination folder.

### Deleting Folders or Bookmarks

1. Single click to highlight the bookmark or folder and then press the delete key on the keyboard.

### Adding a New Bookmark to a Specific Folder

1. Click on "Bookmarks" icon on the upper part of the browser frame.
2. Click on "File," and choose a folder by clicking on one from the drop down menu.

## Bookmarking in Microsoft Internet Explorer

### Adding a Bookmark

1. Click on "Favorites" from the top menu bar.
2. Click on "Add to Favorites."
3. Click "OK."

### Adding a Folder

1. Click on "Favorites" from the top menu bar.
2. Click on "Organize Favorites...".
3. Click on the folder icon that has a starburst pattern on the upper right corner. This will create a new folder for you to name.

### Moving Bookmarks Into Folders

1. Highlight the bookmark and drag it to a new folder.

### Deleting Folders or Bookmarks

1. Highlight folders or bookmarks and use the delete key or the delete button in the window.

### Adding a New Bookmark to a Specific Folder

1. Click on "Favorites" from the top menu bar.
2. Click on "Add to Favorites."
3. Click on the "Create In" button.
4. Click on the destination folder.
5. Click "OK."

# Part 2

# Reference Resources

## Acronyms (*see also* Dictionaries; Reference: Other Virtual Reference Sites)

### Acronym Finder

http://www.acronymfinder.com/

More than 181,000 abbreviations, acronyms and initialisms are contained in this database. One type of search is called "exact acronym" and brings back results only if they match the letters exactly. A second type of search "acronym begins with" brings back all definitions that begin with the letters. A third type "acronym (wildcard)" truncates the acronym on both sides so a search for SPC finds SPC, SPCA, ASPC SPCC and 145 more. A final type of search "reverse lookup (keywords)" searches for acronyms that match the keywords in the definition. Do not use periods in the search (i.e., USA not U.S.A.) unless the acronym normally contains a period (i.e., X.25).

**Authority:** Mountain Data Systems

### The World Wide Web Acronym and Abbreviation Server

http://www.ucc.ie/info/net/acronyms/

This easy-to-use site automatically truncates the search on both the right and left sides. A search for SPCA includes the following results: ASPCA, ISPCA NSPCC and others. It is also searchable by keyword. There are more than 17,000 acronyms and abbreviations included in the database.

**Authority:** Peter Flynn, Webmaster

## Activities for Young Children

### Coloring.Com

http://www.coloring.com/

An online coloring book with pictures relating to holidays, animals, sports and activities. Click on "let's start coloring" to access a list of pictures. Select a color from the palette on the right, then click on a picture to add the color.

**Authority:** Coloring.com

### Crayola

http://www.crayola.com/

This colorful site includes activities, stories, games, coloring pages and crafts. Special sections are available for Educators, Parents and Crayola Kids.

**Authority:** Binney & Smith, Inc.

### Disney.com

http://www.disney.com/

Although this site is extremely commercial, it still has activities to do, stories to read and games to play for all kinds of kids. The main contents of this page are divided into the following sections: Entertainment, Zeether (games and music), Playhouse, Disney Blast, Fun for Families, Vacations and Shopping.

**Authority:** Disney

### Favorite Kid Links

http://www.goodnet.com/~eel/

This is a great web page for kids. It is divided into two sections: Little Kids and Bigger Kids. Each section lists lots of activity websites including Barney, Blue's Clues, Elmo, Pokemon, Rugrats, Theodore Tugboat, Sesame Street and Story Hour. ∞

**Authority:** Unknown

### GameKids

http://www.gamekids.com

This "is a gathering place for kids of all ages to learn and exchange non-computer games and activities. Each month, selected games and rhymes (traditional and contemporary), activities and recipes will be selected from around the world for you to download, print out and play." Click on "Games" to go to the main list. Game types include tag games, water games and world games.

**Authority:** Media Bridge Technologies

### Idea Box

http://www.theideabox.com/

A plethora of activities can be found by clicking on the categories: Idea of the Day, Activities, Seasonal, Games, Music and Songs, Recipes, Craft Recipes and Crafts.

---

∞ : Indicates sites rich in links on website topic.

✐ : Indicates sites with lesson plans.

There are also monthly contests, a newsletter, message boards and a "site of the week."

**Authority:** Group 23 Solutions

### Sesame Street

http://www.sesameworkshop.org/sesame/

The contents of this site are divided up into two categories: Parents and Kids. Within these sections are games, activities, music, stories, television schedules and articles.

**Authority:** Children's Television Workshop

# Almanacs *(see also* Reference: Other Virtual Reference Sites)

### American FactFinder

http://factfinder.census.gov/home/en/whatsinaff.html

This statistic-rich site is a "data access and dissemination system that provides useful facts and information about your community, your economy and your society. The system will find and retrieve the information you need from some of the Census Bureau's largest data sets." It is searchable by subject, keyword, file type and date.

**Authority:** United States Census Bureau

### Information Please Almanac

http://www.infoplease.com/

First published in 1947, the paper version of this almanac is a staple for most libraries. The Web version includes information in the following categories: Daily Almanac, World, United States, History & Gov't, Biography, Sports, Entertainment, Business & Finance, Society & Culture, Health & Science, Weather & Climate and Homework Center.

**Authority:** Information Please LLC

### Information Please Fact Monster

http://www.factmonster.com

The site divides its content into the following sections: World & News, US, People, Word Wise, Science, Math, Sports, Cool Stuff, Games & Quizzes and Homework Center. Entries under each section topic consist of brief factual lists, charts and/or paragraphs. The exception to this is the Homework Center section which is further divided into broad subject categories and topics. Entries here tend to be two-to-five paragraphs in length.

**Authority:** Information Please LLC

### Old Farmers Almanac

http://www.almanac.com

In print since 1792, the almanac has "published useful information for people in all walks of life: tide tables for

those who live near the ocean; sunrise tables and planting charts for those who live on the farm; recipes for those who live in the kitchen; and weather predictions for those who don't like the question of weather left up in the air."

**Authority:** Yankee Publishing Inc.

### Yahooligans! Kids' Almanac

http://www.yahooligans.com/content/ka/index.html

The popular Yahoo! search engine provides this almanac of useful information. The site is divided into large subject categories: Animals, Body & Food, Book Baedeker, Business & Technology, Creature Catalog, Disaster Digest, Environment Examination, Laws & Rights, Measuring Up, People Pamphlet, Speaking of Language, Sports Section, Universal Knowledge, The Wide World of War and The World. Each of these categories is divided into subject listings of links to information created by Yahooligans!. Charts, descriptive paragraphs, illustrations and links to other web sources are available for each subdivision.

**Authority:** Yahoo! and Yahooligans!

# American Sign Language

### American Sign Language Browser

http://commtechlab.msu.edu/sites/aslweb/

A staggering number of ASL signs are available on this site through written description and in the Quicktime Video format. Browse through the alphabetically arranged list of words and concepts.

**Authority:** Communication Technology Laboratory, Michigan State University

### American Sign Language Fingerspelling

http://www.where.com/scott.net/asl/

The site includes a standard dictionary to learn the basic fingershapes, a fingerspelling converter and an interactive quiz.

**Authority:** Scott Gaertner

### Deaf Resource Library

http://www.deaflibrary.org/

The site mission is to create an online "collection of reference material and links intended to educate and inform people about Deaf cultures in Japan and the United States." Scroll down the page to access the directory of linked resources. The sources here include organizations, linguistics, resources for deaf kids, interpreting, news and more.

**Authority:** Karen Nakamura

## Handspeak: Online Sign Language Dictionary

http://www.handspeak.com/

Spun off from the Deaf World Web, this site is a great resource for learning Sign Language. Signs are organized in alphabetical order and categories such as animals and colors. Other lists include different types of sign language such as baby and international and features such as stories in sign language.

**Authority:** Jolanta A. Lapiak

# Archaeology (*see also* History; Mythology; Religion)

## Archaeological Fieldwork Opportunities

http://www.cincpac.com/afos/testpit.html

Click on a geographic region on the image map or select a place from the list of links at the bottom of the page to begin searching this site. Entries "on this list may or may not offer credit, remuneration, room or board. In many cases volunteer opportunities require significant payment for participation, as well as travel costs to the site. Caveat emptor." Still, if you are trying to become involved in archaeology or just want to take an interesting vacation this is a fun place to search. Listings for the previous year are archived.

**Authority:** Ken Stuart of Cornell University

## Archaeology on the Net

http://www.serve.com/archaeology/

Hundreds of archeological resources are arranged under three broad categories: Regional, Resources and General. Within these categories are links to associations, museums, teaching resources, country-specific archaeological web pages, underwater archaeology and more. The links listed in the gray box connect to books for sale at Amazon.com. ⚭

**Authority:** Archaeology on the Net

## ArchNet

http://archnet.asu.edu/

Part of the World Wide Web Virtual Library, this site indexes archaeology related websites. Extensive help screens are available to assist you in using the site. It is organized into sections including Regional View, Subject Areas, Academic Depts, Museums, News, Journals & Publishers and Q&A. It is browsable by geographic region or subject area and can be searched by keyword. ⚭

**Authority:** Thomas Plunkett and Jonathan Lizee; Arleyn Simon and Jim Ames

## Voyage into Archaeology

http://ted.educ.sfu.ca/people/staff/jmd/archaeology /voyage1.htm

There are many resources on this site including activities, a glossary, curriculum ideas and other web-based resources. The "activities were designed so that as you go through them, you'll be making the same decisions and asking yourself the same questions that an archaeologist would ask. By going through the activities you're taking the first step to learn more about becoming an archaeologist." (Grades 3–12)

**Authority:** by Jacqueline Dale and Mike Bowen of the Faculty of Education, Simon Fraser University

# Architecture (*see also* Art; Museums)

## archINFORM

http://www.archinform.net/

Click on either English or Deutsch to begin using this enormous database in the language of your choice. The site states that there are "over 9500 built and unrealized projects from various architects and planners. The architecture of the 20th century is the main theme of this database. It's possible to look for a special project via an architect, town or keyword with the indices or by using a query form. For most entries you get the name, address, keywords and information about further literature. Some entries include images, comments, links to other Websites or internal links. Projects with images are marked with a 'mediaball' in the indices."

**Authority:** Sascha Hendel, Timm Knief and Katja Melan

## Architectronics Studio

http://darkwing.uoregon.edu/~struct/

The site preface states that "all of the material contained within this multi-media work has been developed by the authors over decades of practice and teaching. The site contains lectures, example problems, case studies, structural typologies, essays, links, animations, movies, suggested readings and more." The site is divided into two sections, resources and courseware. These sections access the same material. Resources are arranged by type such as Essays, Articles and Links; and Interactive Teaching Tools. Courseware is arranged by topic such as Pencil Towers and the History and Development of the High-Rise.

**Authority:** Chris H. Luebkeman, in collaboration with University of Oregon NewMedia Center, with the cooperation of University Computing and the Department of Architecture

### Architecture through the Ages

http://library.thinkquest.org/10098/

Maya, Aztec, Greek and Egyptian structures are some of the cultures covered on this Think Quest sponsored website. "You will learn how certain cultures built their homes, temples and cities. You may also learn a little about their religion, how they lived every day and more." (Grades 6–9)

**Authority:** Shane Goldmacher, James Arndt and Alexander Lee

### archKIDecture

http://www.archkidecture.org/

There are five main sections on this site: About Architects, About Structures, News & Links, Become an Architect and Build it Yourself. The most completed section, About Structures, opens with a group of architectural photos and illustrations. Click on any of them to get more information about building materials, building styles and other architectural elements. (Grades 3–7)

**Authority:** Julie Cowan

### Built in America

http://memory.loc.gov/ammem/hhhtml/hhhome.html

Digital images enhance the Library of Congress' HABS/HAER Catalog. The catalog is searchable by keyword or browsable by subject or geographic region. "The Historic American Buildings Survey (HABS) and the Historic American Engineering Record (HAER) ... collections document achievements in architecture, engineering and design in the United States and its territories through a comprehensive range of building types and engineering technologies, including examples as diverse as windmills, one-room schoolhouses, the Golden Gate Bridge and buildings designed by Frank Lloyd Wright." The Built in America site is part of the American Memory Project.

**Authority:** Library of Congress

### Castles on the Web

http://www.castlesontheweb.com/

Scroll down this page to get to an astonishing collection of links, photographs and information. Links are annotated and rated to make them easier to use. The contents of this site are divided into the following categories: Introduction, Castle Greetings! Castle Tours, Castle Collections, Palaces and Great Homes, Abbeys and Churches, Castle Photo Archive, Miscellaneous Castles, Castles for Kids, Glossary of Terms, Castle Quest, Site of the Day, Castle Books, Medieval Studies

Heraldry, Myths and Legends, Related Organizations and Weapons and Supplies.

**Authority:** Castles on the Web

### Cities/Buildings Database

http://www.washington.edu/ark2/

According to the site, "the Database was conceived as a multi-disciplinary resource for students, faculty and others in the academic community. It has grown steadily since then, with contributions from a wide range of scholars, and now contains over 5000 images ranging from New York to Central Asia, from African villages, to the Parc de la Villette and conceptual sketches and models of Frank Gehry's Experience Music Project. These have all been scanned from original slides or drawn from documents in the public domain. They are freely available to anyone with access to the Web for use in the classroom, student study or for individual research purposes." The database is both browsable and searchable by Title, Site, Detail, City, State, Nation, Keyword and more. The keyword search function is called "Across All Fields."

**Authority: Authority:** Meredith L. Clausen, Professor Architectural History, University of Washington

### Great Buildings Collection

http://www.greatbuildings.com/

Although the web page is used to promote sales of the CR-ROM, there is still a great deal of free content. The page states that it is a "gateway to architecture around the world and across history documenting a thousand buildings and hundreds of leading architects, with 3D models, photographic images and architectural drawings, commentaries, bibliographies, web links and more, for famous designers and structures of all kinds."

**Authority:** Artifice Inc.

## Arts (*see also* Architecture; Museums, Optical Illusion)

### Art Images for Teaching

http://www.mcad.edu/AICT/html/

This site is divided into the following categories: Ancient, Medieval Era, Renaissance & Baroque, 18th–20th Century and Non-Western art. The images have been selected from photo CDs which are available for loan from this site. (Grades K–12)

**Authority:** Allan T. Kohl of the Minneapolis College of Art and Design

## The Art Room

http://www.arts.ufl.edu/art/rt_room/

"The Art Room is designed around the idea of 'activity' centers that encourage kids to create, to learn and to explore new ideas, places and things on their own." There are six areas to explore on this site: they include: Artrageous Thinking, Library, Artifacts, Gallery, Art Sparkers, Links and What's News. There is also a category called Art Teaching Resources with links to articles, ideas and more websites. (Grades 3–12)

**Authority:** Craig Roland, Associate Professor, Art Education, University of Florida, Gainsville.

## Artcyclopedia

http://www.artcyclopedia.com/

The Artcyclopedia's mission is "to become the definitive and most effective guide to museum-quality fine art on the Internet." The index is restricted to websites where artists' works can be viewed online. The majority of the entries are for painting and sculpture, though they do include other media. To access the 24,000+ links, search for Artists by Name, Artworks by Title or Art Museums by Name/Place. Alternately, you can browse by Movement (e.g. Pop Art, Impressionism), Medium (e.g. sculptors, illustrators), Subject (e.g. landscape painters), Nationality, Name, alphabetically or all women artists. ∞

**Authority:** John Malyon

## ArtLex

http://www.artlex.com/

A dictionary of art terms includes definitions for more than 3,300 terms, "along with thousands of images, pronunciation notes, great quotations and links to other resources on the Web" arranged alphabetically. The dictionary includes a pronunciation guide and a bibliography.

**Authority:** Michael Delahunt, M.F.A.

## ArtsEdNet

http://www.getty.edu/artsednet/home.html

ArtsEdNet's "online service developed by the Getty Education Institute for the Arts, supports the needs of the K–12 arts education community. It focuses on helping arts educators, general classroom teachers using the arts in their curriculum, museum educators and university faculty involved in the arts." Information is arranged into the following sections: Lesson Plans & Curriculum Ideas, Image Galleries, ArtsEdNet Talk, Web Links, Reading Room & Publications and Search & Index. The site is browsable using Site Map or Index or you can use the search engine to search the website. (Grades K–12)

**Authority:** Getty Education Institute for the Arts

## exCALENDAR

http://www.excalendar.net/

Though it is titled the "official exhibition calendar of the world's leading art museums," the database currently contains only 100 or so museums in the database. The site can be searched by keyword, city, exhibition title, artist's name or museum name. There is also a geographic list and an alphabetical list of museums in the database. The entry for each museum includes an address, active link to the museum website, exhibition title and dates. Frequently the entry will also include links for forthcoming exhibits and links to exhibit descriptions. This site will probably grow with time.

**Authority:** Art Museum Network

## Gateway to Art History

http://www.harbrace.com/art/gardner/

Written and designed as a companion to the book "Gardner's Art Through the Ages," this site has indexed art history information on the Internet. Both Student and Instructor categories contain General Resources and Chapter Resources. The Chapter Resources are arranged chronologically with links to study guides, maps, interactive quizzes, images, criticism and information resources. ∞

**Authority:** Chris Witcombe, Professor of Art History, Sweet Briar College

## Incredible Art Department: Favorite Lessons

http://www.artswire.org/kenroar/lessons/lessons.html

This fun site has selected "some great art lessons and projects that you might be interested in doing for your art class or projects that students just may want to do at home." It is arranged into the following areas: Early Childhood Lessons, Elementary Lessons, Jr High/Middle School Lessons, High School Lessons, Undergraduate Lessons, More Lessons, Drama and Art and Art Test. (Grades K–12 and Undergraduate)

**Authority:** Paul Bradley and Ken Rohrer

## KinderArt: Lessons

http://www.bconnex.net/~jarea/lessons.htm

Self-billed as the "Largest Collection of Free Art Lessons on the Internet" this site has hundreds of lesson plans for kids of all ages. The overall goal is to promote art education and communication between parents, educators, artists and students.

**Authority:** KinderArt

### Mark Harden's Artchive

http://www.artchive.com/

Click on "The Artchive" to begin using this site. The following page has an alphabetical list of links down the left side and includes artists, styles and regions. There are more than 2,000 images from more than 200 different artists in the database. ∞

**Authority:** Mark Harden

### Voice of the Shuttle: Web Page for Humanities Research

http://vos.ucsb.edu/

The number of sites linked to this page is amazing. The mission of the Voice of the Shuttle "has been to provide a structured and briefly annotated guide to online resources that at once respects the established humanities disciplines in their professional organization and points toward the transformation of those disciplines as they interact with the sciences and social sciences and with new digital media." The site is keyword-searchable. ∞

**Authority:** Alan Liu, English Department, University of California, Santa Barbara

### World Wide Arts Resources

http://www.wwar.com/

This extraordinary site provides comprehensive access to arts on the Internet. It is divided into five broad categories: Search the Arts, Artist Portfolios, Arts News, Marketplace and Services. The site is keyword-searchable and a tiny link at the bottom of the page titled Browse the Arts allows you to browse through the site categories. ∞

**Authority:** World Wide Arts Resource, Corp.

## Associations (*see also* Library Associations)

### ASAE Gateway to Associations

http://www.asaenet.org/Gateway/OnlineAssocSlist.html

Information for hundreds of associations are indexed on this site. Use the drop down box to access the Gateway to Organizations. The Gateway is searchable by Association Name Contains, Category Keyword, City or State. Results retrieve lists of associations with links to their websites. ∞

**Authority:** American Society of Association Executives

### AssociationCentral.com

http://associationcentral.com/

A membership is required to be listed in this directory. The directory is searchable by keyword or browsable by the following categories: Arts & Humanities, Business & Economy, Computing & Internet, Education, Entertainment, Government, Health, News & Media, Recreation & Sports, Science, Social Science and Society & Culture. ∞

**Authority:** AssociationCentral.com

### IPL Associations

http://www.ipl.org/ref/AON/

Part of the Internet Public Library website, this page includes "over 1100 Internet sites providing information about a wide variety of professional and trade associations, cultural and art organizations, political parties and advocacy groups, labor unions, academic societies and research institutions." The links are organized into subject areas. The database is also browsable by title and searchable by keyword. ∞

**Authority:** Internet Public Library

## Astronomy (*see also* Physics; Science; Science Fair)

### Astronomy Picture of the Day

http://antwrp.gsfc.nasa.gov/apod/astropix.html

"Each day a different image or photograph of our fascinating universe is featured, along with a brief explanation written by a professional astronomer." This site has been online since 1995 and contains the "largest collection of annotated astronomical images on the Internet." The archive is searchable by keyword. There is also a picture subject index.

**Authority:** Laboratory for High-Energy Astrophysics (LHEA), NASA, Goddard Space Flight Center (GSFC) and Michigan Technological University

### Astronomy Unbound

http://www.herts.ac.uk/astro_ub/

Useful for both high school and undergraduate students, this site is a virtual astronomy textbook. It is arranged in chapters and then sections such as The Solar System, Inside the Sun, Dark Matter and The Nature of Galaxies. The sections themselves consist of essays written for this site or links to other sites. (High School–Undergraduate)

**Authority:** Professor Jim Hough, Ian Williams, University of Hertfordshire

### Center for Science Education at UC Berkeley Space Sciences Laboratory

http://cse.ssl.berkeley.edu/

There are so many valuable resources on this page for teaching physics that it would be impossible to list them all. They are grouped under three main sections. The first and default page is titled "Public" and has resources on general topics such as At Home Astronomy and Sunspots. The second section is titled "Educators" and contains links, lesson plans, activities and other educational material. The third section, "Scientists," includes outreach projects and links for scientists. (Grades K–Undergraduate) ∞ ✎

**Authority:** Space Science Laboratory, University of California Berkeley

### The Nine Planets: A Multimedia Tour of the Solar System

http://seds.lpl.arizona.edu/nineplanets/nineplanets/nineplanets.html

This award-winning website is "an overview of the history, mythology and current scientific knowledge of each of the planets and moons in our solar system. Each page has text and images, some have sounds and movies, most provide references to additional related information." The virtual handbook includes the sun, planets, moons, comets, asteroids and other objects. (Grades 4–12)

**Authority:** Bill Arnett

### StarChild: A Learning Center for Young Astronomers

http://starchild.gsfc.nasa.gov/docs/StarChild/StarChild.html

A great web page to use for teaching astronomy, this NASA-sponsored site has been arranged into two levels of difficulty. These levels include the same categories: Solar System, Universe, Space Stuff and Glossary. Level two expands on the content of level one. There are a large number of activities, sound files, movies and text on this page. It is searchable and contains a list of related websites. (Grades 2–7)

**Authority:** Dr. Laura A. Whitlock, StarChild Project Leader and High Energy Astrophysics Science Archive Research Center (HEASARC)

### WWW-Virtual Library: Astronomy & Astrophysics

http://webhead.com/WWWVL/Astronomy/

Scroll through this site to find a subject list which include: Observations, Data, Publications, People organizations, Software, Research Areas of Astronomy, Various Lists of Astronomy, Astronomical Imagery, Education,

History and Miscellaneous. Below this list, is the access point to the master database which indexes all of the websites included under the subject categories. This database contains almost 3,000 records. ∞

**Authority:** AstroWeb Consortium

## Atlases and Maps (*see also* Flags; Travel)

### Atlapedia Online

http://www.atlapedia.com/

The Atlapedia site has almanac-type information and maps under two headings: Countries A to Z and World Maps. Countries A to Z offers alphabetically arranged access to facts, figures and statistics relating to specific countries. World Maps accesses two world maps, one political and the other physical. Clicking on the political map will bring up a list of countries to choose from. After choosing a country another map will appear. This map shows cities, bordering countries and states. This page also has a cross link to the country's physical map. If you choose the physical map first, it will bring up a list of countries to choose from. After choosing a country, another map appears a relief map showing mountains, rivers, valleys and other terrain. This page has a cross link to the political map.

**Authority:** Latimer Clarke Corporation

### InfoNation

http://www.un.org/Pubs/CyberSchoolBus/infonation/e_infonation.htm

The United Nations Statistics Division has provided all of the content on this site except for the languages. According to the site: "InfoNation is an easy-to-use, two-step database that allows you to view and compare the most up-to-date statistical data for the Member States of the United Nations. In [the] first menu, you can select up to seven countries. Then, you can proceed to the data menu where you will be able to select statistics and other data fields."

**Authority:** United Nations Statistics Division

### MapQuest

http://www.mapquest.com

One of the most popular atlases on the Internet, this interactive site allows you to search for maps, get detailed driving directions and plan a road trip. Not all cities have street-level maps, but a surprising number do. To start, search for any of the following: address, city, state, province, country or zip code. The site also provides yellow pages and travel guides.

**Authority:** MapQuest

### National Atlas of the United States of America

http://www.nationalatlas.gov/

Use this site by clicking on Atlas Maps to locate and map more than 2,000,000 geographic names in the United States. The maps are organized into four categories: Interactive Maps, Multimedia Maps, Printed Maps and Map Layers Data Warehouse.

**Authority:** United States Department of the Interior

### National Geographic's Map Machine

http://www.nationalgeographic.com/resources/ngo/maps/

While there are a lot of really great dynamic maps and resources on this page, the complexity of navigation and the overwhelming number of resources can be daunting. Click on "Map Machine" to access the dynamic maps. These maps are keyword-searchable or browsable by categories such as World Themes, Historical Maps and Mars.

**Authority:** National Geographic

### Odden's Bookmarks, The Fascinating World of Maps and Mapping

http://oddens.geog.uu.nl/index.html

Boasting more than 14,000 cartographic links, this site really does index the Internet world of maps. It is searchable by keyword, country or category such as libraries or map collections. There are thirteen categories to browse through including: Maps and Atlases, Government Cartography, Gazetteers, Search Engines and Touristic Sites.

**Authority:** Mr. Oddens, KartLab UU

### OSSHE Historical Atlas Resource Library

http://www.uoregon.edu/~atlas/

Currently the maps on this site are exclusively from Europe, the Middle East, North Africa and North America. Many of the maps are interactive and require the shockwave plugin. "This project was designed to provide a corpus of material for use by faculty in many fields and on many campuses within the OSSHE system to enhance the learning experience for students." Along with the maps are many pictures or images of the country.

**Authority:** Dept. of History, New Media Center and Dept. of Geography InfoGraphics Lab

### University of Oregon Rare Map Collection

http://scarlett.libs.uga.edu/darchive/hargrett/maps/maps.html

An impressive archive of historical maps covering the New World, Colonial America, Revolutionary America, Union and Expansion, the Civil War and more. Maps of Georgia comprise a large section of this archive with maps of cities and coastal areas, Revolutionary War maps and other historical maps.

**Authority:** Hargrett Rare Book and Manuscript Library, University of Georgia Libraries

### U.S. Census Bureau's Mapping and Cartographic Resources

http://tiger.census.gov/

Many different map resources are available on this page. All of the maps rely on census data. Use the TIGER mapping service to generate your own maps based on various criteria. Under "Frequently Requested Resources" is a State and County QuickFacts category where you can find basic statistics for states and counties such as population and economic indicators.

**Authority:** United States Census Bureau

# Biography (*see also* Full-Text Resources; History; Prizes and Awards)

### Author Webliography

http://www.lib.lsu.edu/hum/authors.html

The home page states that "this directory is an index of indexes. It contains pointers to individual author guides or other cumulative documents that deal with specific writers. Admittedly, most of these authors are "literary." I have not included many authors from genres such as science fiction or romance." The site can be browsed by author's last name. ∞

**Authority:** Steven R. Harris, University Libraries, Louisiana State University

### Authors on the Web

http://www.people.Virginia.EDU/~jbh/author.html

"This page is an attempt to bring together literary author biographies available on the World Wide Web. The biographies vary in quality, timeliness, length and authority." The site is arranged in alphabetical order by last name and is updated frequently. ∞

**Authority:** Bonnie Hanks

## The Biographical Dictionary

http://www.s9.com/biography/

The database has more than 28,000 biographies. It is international in scope but focuses primarily on European and American historical figures. The entries vary in length from one line to one paragraph and contain dates and facts.

**Authority:** S9.com

## Biographical Directory of the United States Congress, 1774 to Present

http://bioguide.congress.gov/

Over 13,000 members of the National Legislature and Continental Congress are included in the database. Entries include dates, facts, bibliography and related research collections. The database is searchable by name or state.

**Authority:** Senate Historical Office and Legislative Resource Center of the House of Representatives

## Biographies of Women Mathematicians

http://www.agnesscott.edu/lriddle/women/women.htm

This growing site indexes biographical essays which include a biographical sketch, a bibliography and frequently a picture or illustration. Entries are listed in alphabetical order by name or in chronological order by date.

**Authority:** Mathematics Students, Agnes Scott College

## Biography.com

http://www.biography.com/

Sponsored by the popular A&E show, "Biography," this site offers a searchable index to over 25,000 biographies. Use the format "lastname, firstname" to search the database. Entries vary in size but most are a single paragraph in length.

**Authority:** Arts & Entertainment Network

## Celebrating Women's History

http://www.gale.com/freresrc/womenhst/index.htm

Although there are only 60+ biographies linked on this site, the entries are well written and quite extensive. Other interesting additions to the site are Activities, Links, Trials, a Timeline of Key Events in Women's History and a Quiz to Test Your Women's History Savvy.

**Authority:** Gale Publications

## Contributions of 20th Century Women to Physics

http://www.physics.ucla.edu/~cwp/

The focus on this page is limited to twentieth century women who made contributions in physics before 1976. To find an entry look through the photo gallery, search the archives by name or choose a field and a name. Each article is quite extensive including bibliographies, publications, contributions and honors.

**Authority:** Nina Byers and Colleagues, Physics Dept., University of California, Los Angeles

## Distinguished Women of Past and Present

http://www.distinguishedwomen.com/

Hundreds of biographies are available at this site. Some of the biographies actually reside on other sites. Find the entries by field of expertise or by name. Entries vary in length and detail.

**Authority:** Danuta Bois

## Faces of Science: African Americans in the Sciences

http://www.princeton.edu/~mcbrown/display/faces.html

"Profiled here are African American men and women who have contributed to the advancement of science and engineering." This site is browsable by name, by scientific field or by profession. Each entry includes a brief biographical sketch, bibliography and other information such as awards and memberships.

**Authority:** Mitchell C. Brown, Princeton

## 4000 Years of Women in Science

http://www.astr.ua.edu/4000WS/4000WS.html

Covering a large time period, this site is sectioned into four content areas: Introduction, Photographs, Biographies and References. The Introduction contains information about the history of women as scientists and the "whys" of this site. The Photographs section is arranged by site of origin and then alphabetically. The Biographies section opens to an alphabetical list, but there are links to a chronological list and a field of study list. The biographies range from a single sentence for Sonduk (C. 630 B.C.E.) to six or so paragraphs for Marie Curie (1867-1934). The References section is a list of print sources which were used in preparing these pages.

**Authority:** Dept. of Physics and Astronomy, The University of Alabama

## Invention Dimension: Inventor of the Week Archives

http://web.mit.edu/invent/www/archive.html

To find an inventor or invention browse through the alphabetical lists or try the search engine. The entries are three to seven paragraphs in length and contain a picture of the inventor and other illustrations.

**Authority:** James Fergason, Massachusetts Institute of Technology

## Lives, The Biography Resource

http://amillionlives.com/

Instead of providing biographies, this site indexes and links to hundreds of other websites. Included among the links are "biographies, autobiographies, memoirs, diaries, letters, narratives oral histories and more. Individual lives of the famous, the infamous and the not so famous. Group biographies about people who share a common profession, historical era or geography. Also general collections, resources on biographical criticism and special collections." ∞

**Authority:** Simplelives.com

## National Inventors Hall of Fame

http://www.invent.org/book/index.html

The inductees to this Hall of Fame are listed in four indexes: Inventors (alphabetical index), Index of Inventions, Timeline of Inventors/Inventions and Inventors (by date of induction). The entries for the inventors include a picture and four to nine paragraphs of biographical text. This site is searchable by keyword.

**Authority:** National Inventors Hall of Fame

## Presidents of the United States

http://www.ipl.org/ref/POTUS

Articles include biographical background information, election results, cabinet members, presidency highlights and miscellaneous facts on each of the presidents. Each entry contains links to biographies, historical documents, audio files, video files and other presidential sites.

**Authority:** Internet Public Library

## Voices from the Gaps: Women Writers of Color

http://voices.cla.umn.edu/

Over 100 biographies are organized by name, birthplace, ethnicity and date. Database entries include biographical information, works by the author, works about the author and related links.

**Authority:** Voices From the Gaps Editorial Board

## WWW Virtual Library for the History of Science, Technology & Medicine: Biographical Sources

http://www.asap.unimelb.edu.au/hstm/hstm_biographical.htm

A comprehensive index of biographical information on the web as it relates to Science, Technology & Medicine also lists biographical sources, exhibitions and institutions. It includes a search engine and can be browsed by alphabetic list and scientific field.

**Authority:** Tim Sherratt

# Biology (*see also* Botany and Agriculture; Paleontology; Zoology)

## Biology Project

http://www.biology.arizona.edu/

Developed by the University of Arizona, the Biology Project is designed for both college and high school students. The site is rich with activities, articles, tutorials, self tests and projects, some of which are in Spanish. There are many topics here such as metabolism, biochemistry, cell biology, lung toxicology, genetics and immunology. According to the site, "students will find that the information covered in The Biology Project is probably just what they've been studying in their introductory biology course and advanced students will find these materials to be a useful review. All students will benefit from the real-life applications of biology and the inclusion of up-to-date research findings." (High School–Undergraduate)

**Authority:** The Biology Project, University of Arizona

## Cell and Molecular Biology Online

http://www.cellbio.com/

Although the emphasis of this site is on cell and molecular biology, many of the resources are more general in nature. Links are arranged into sections such as Research, Education, Communication and Random. Check out the links under Cool Bio Stuff for interactive sites such as Cells Alive! at http://www.cellsalive.com/. ∞

**Authority:** Pamela M. Gannon, Ph.D.

## Classification of Living Things

http://anthro.palomar.edu/animal/

This is a tutorial about the "Linnaean system of classification used in the biological sciences to describe and categorize all living things. The focus is on finding out how humans fit within this system. In addition, you will discover part of the great diversity of life forms and come to understand why some animals are considered to be close to us in their evolutionary history." The tutorial is just one of a larger set of anthropological tutorials found at: http://anthro.palomar.edu/tutorials/ (See "Social Science" for more information). (High School–Undergraduate)

**Authority:** Dennis O'Neil, Ph.D., Palomar College

## Cool Science for Curious Kids

http://www.hhmi.org/coolscience/

The goal of this site is to "help your child appreciate science." There are currently five different science activities of varying length and complexity. These activities include edible plants, stuff we breath, butterflies and caterpillars, snakes, lizards, monkeys and moose and miniature world without microscope. (Grades K–3)

**Authority:** Howard Hughes Medical Institute

## Just for Kids

http://mbgnet.mobot.org/

This simple site helps kids study biomes which are regions of the world with specific types of plants and animals. The resources are grouped into three large categories Biomes of the World, Freshwater Ecosystems and Marine Ecosystems are incredible pages with tons of articles, links and pictures. (Grades 3–8)

**Authority:** The Evergreen Project Inc.

## Ken's Bio-Web Resources

http://www.hoflink.com/~house/

Indexing over 3,400 sites on the Internet, this website is a great place to start looking for biological information. The initial page is divided into the following sections: Animals (Anatomy/Physiology, Behavior), Cell Sites (Chemistry, Structure/Function), Ecology, Evolution, General Biology Reference Sources, Genetic Sites (Mendelian, Molecular), Human Physiology, Microbiology, Plant Physiology and Aquatic and Marine Biology.

**Authority:** Ken House

## Kimball's Biology Pages

http://www.ultranet.com/~jkimball/BiologyPages/

The Biology Pages are created by Dr. John W. Kimball, a retired Harvard professor. They "represent an online biology textbook consisting of: alphabetized lists of biological terms (the index/glossary) with links to discussions, often illustrated, of a wide range of biological topics." Much of this information has been drawn from Dr. Kimball's Biology text, specifically the sixth edition (1994). (High School–Undergraduate)

**Authority:** Dr. John W. Kimball

## National Biological Information Infrastructure

http://www.nbii.gov/

Information on this site is created by various government agencies, academic institutions, non-government organizations and private industry. The main goal is to provide "increased access to data and information on the nation's biological resources." Resources are categorized under Current Biological Issues, Biological Disciplines, Geographic Perspectives, Teacher Resources and Data & Information Resources. The site is keyword-searchable and has a comprehensive site map/index.

**Authority:** The Center for Biological Informatics of the U.S. Geological Survey

## Nature and Wildlife Field Guides

http://www.enature.com/guides/select_group.asp

The contents of this site are from the best-selling National Audubon Society Field Guides, Regional Guides, Nature Guides and Birds Interactive CD-ROM, published by Alfred A. Knopf, Inc, Published and Produced by Chanticleer Press. There are five main sections on the site. Field Guides is the opening page and features over 4,800 plants and animals categorized into: Amphibians, Birds, Butterflies, Fishes, Insects, Mammals, Reptiles, Seashells, Seashore Creatures, Spiders, Trees and Wildflowers. Local Guides is the next section and my personal favorite. It allows the input of your zipcode and e-mail address and then produces lists of species that are native or found in your region. Bird Song is the middle section and includes audio files of more than 550 birds. Birding Basics is fourth and discusses all of the basics for becoming a bird watching enthusiast. Finally, Ask an Expert is an Internet community where you can post your travel notes, discuss nature topics and ask experts for more information. They maintain a list of frequently asked questions (FAQ) and previously asked questions. These guides are created for North America.

**Authority:** The National Audubon Society and eNature.com

## UCMP Glossary

http://www.ucmp.berkeley.edu/glossary/glossary.html

Dictionaries for the language of biology are found here. They include Volume 1: Phylogenetics, Volume 2: Geology, Volume 3: Biochemistry, Volume 4: Cell Biology, Volume 5: Ecology, Volume 6: Life History, Volume 7: Zoology and Volume 8: Botany. The contents of the volumes are arranged in alphabetical order. Entries are one to two sentences long and include cross links to related terms.

**Authority:** Museum of Paleontology, University of California

# Books (*see also* Full-Text Resources; Reading and Literature)

### abebooks.com

http://dogbert.abebooks.com/

Independent booksellers from around the world participate in this site. The database of more than 28 million used, rare and out-of-print books is searchable by keyword, title and/or author.

**Authority:** Advanced Book Exchange, Inc. and abebooks.com

### Alibris

http://www.alibris.com

Use this site to search for out of print books. Alibris can be used to purchase books, verify citations or to search by subject for possible interlibrary loans. Thousands of booksellers now have their holdings online here. Find a book and Alibris will "retrieve it, whether it's from a tiny Alaskan bookshop or plucked from our own shelves."

**Authority:** Alibris

### Amazon.com

http://www.amazon.com

Amazon.com supposedly has the "Earth's biggest selection of products, including free electronic greeting cards, online auctions and millions of books, CDs, videos, DVDs, toys and games and electronics." The bookstore gives current prices, full bibliographic citations and frequently includes book reviews, tables of contents and other information. The database is searchable by author, title, subject, keyword and ISBN. Amazon.com also includes bestseller lists, award lists, articles and interviews. You can now buy and sell used books through the Amazon service.

**Authority:** Amazon.com

### Antiqbook

http://www.antiqbook.com/

Click on "The NAN searchable databases" to access the catalog of used, rare and out-of-print books. Antiqbook is a network of many booksellers throughout Europe.

**Authority:** Antiqbook

### Barnes & Noble

http://www.barnesandnoble.com/

The well-known bricks and mortar store has an easy to use online store which sells books, music, DVDs and videos, video games, textbooks, bargain books and e-books. Entries include the full bibliographic citation and book reviews. One unique feature of this site is the store finder. Enter your zip code in the search box and find the closest Barnes & Noble.

**Authority:** Barnes and Noble

### Book Sale Finder

http://www.Book-Sales-in-America.com/

Just click on one of the states and find out where the book sales are going on locally. Most of the entries are run by non-profit organizations, but book fair organizers and for-profit dealers are allowed to advertise here. The "for-profits" are clearly marked.

**Authority:** Book Sale Finder

### Bookfinder

http://www.bookfinder.com/

The site says it is "The ultimate resource for book shoppers! Over 30 million new, used, rare and out of print books at your fingertips..." More than 30,000 different used bookstores participate in this website.

**Authority:** 13th Generation Media

### Books On Tape

http://www.booksontape.com/

Originally founded in 1975, Books on Tape's purpose is to rent/sell best-selling books on tape. It does a wonderful job of providing a searchable database of books on tape that can be interlibrary loaned or purchased. The service can be searched by keyword, title, author or genre.

**Authority:** Books On Tape

### BookWebSites

http://www.bookwebsites.com/

There are more than 120,000 book-related sites in this index. It includes online books and magazines, libraries, newspapers, literary agents, writing resources, comic books, booksellers and publishers. The site is searchable by keyword or browsable via the 5,400+ subject categories. A companion site, BookPricer, was created to find the best price on a book. Go to http://www.bookpricer.com/

**Authority:** BookSearchEngine, Inc.

### Bookwire

http://www.bookwire.com/

While many of the sources listed on Bookwire are fee-based, there are many free or partially free. The goal of this site is to be "THE comprehensive online portal into the book industry. Our mission is to provide librarians, publishers, booksellers, authors and general book enthusiasts with the resources they need." The resources include standards such as Library Journal, Boston Book Review, ALA and more.

**Authority:** RR Bowker, Reed Elsevier, Inc.

## IBCA: International Book Collectors Association

http://www.rarebooks.org/

The major categories on this site include: To Collect, To Inform, Popular Pages, To Educate and To Preserve. Within these categories are a host of resources on book appraisal, rare books, book collecting, first edition identification, points of issue, prize winning books and more.

**Authority:** International Book Collectors Association

## Shoenhof's Foreign Books

http://www.schoenhofs.com/

Shoenhof's has been in business since 1856. It offers the "largest selection of foreign-language books in North America." Included in its catalog are books in "over 500 languages and dialects, as well as fiction, nonfiction and children's books in 30 languages." It is searchable by author, title or ISBN and browsable by fiction, nonfiction, language learning and children's books.

**Authority:** Shoenhof's

## 21 North Main

http://www.21northmain.com/

This site is a "virtual marketplace for used books; the first choice for anyone seeking to buy used, out-of-print, antiquarian or rare books. Use our simple search function. Browse the millions of volumes in our online database for a single volume or an entire library." It is highly recommended by one of the collection development librarians at Idaho State University. Searching is done by keyword, author or title, or by browsing their "bookshelves."

**Authority:** 21 North Main

## Writer's Toolbox

http://www.writerstoolbox.com/

This is a wonderful resource for writers. Brian Pomeroy, editor of the book BeginnerNet, began the "Writer's Toolbox in 1996 out of [his] own need to collect and organize online writing resources. [He] created it and maintains it simply because [he] like[s] sharing these excellent resources with others." Included on the page are links to resources in the following categories: Essentials, Reference, Fiction, Drama, Tech

Writing, PR/Promotion, Journalism, Research, Business/Markets/Jobs, Software and Creativity. ∞

**Authority:** Brian Pomeroy

# Botany and Agriculture (*see also* Biology; Science; Science Fairs)

## AGRICOLA

http://www.nal.usda.gov/ag98/

The National Agricultural Library's database includes citations to articles, books and other resources. The site states that it covers "all aspects of agriculture and allied disciplines, including plant and animal sciences, forestry, entomology, soil and water resources, agricultural economics, agricultural engineering, agricultural products, alternative farming practices and food and nutrition."(High School–Researcher)

**Authority:** The National Agricultural Library

## Botany for Kids

http://www.nbii.gov/disciplines/botany/kids.html

Sponsored by the National Biological Information Infrastructure, this site links to botany science projects and activities especially for grades 3–8. In broader terms the site indexes many botany resources in categories such as Plant Biology and Gardening. (Grades 3–8) ∞

**Authority:** National Biological Information Infrastructure

## Botany WWW Sites

http://www.botany.org/bsa/www-bot.html

Arranged in a simple subject list, Botany WWW Sites includes many wonderful, authoritative resources. It is part of the larger Botanical Society of America site. ∞

**Authority:** Botanical Society of America

## The Garden Gate

http://garden-gate.prairienet.org/

This extensive collection of evaluated and annotated links is organized into the following nine sections: Reading Room, Teaching Garden, Garden Shop, Sun Room, Down the Garden Path..., Mailing Lists, Newsgroups and Web Forums, Holding Bed and Gardening in Illinois. ∞

**Authority:** Karen Fletcher

## Internet Directory for Botany

http://www.botany.net/IDB/

More than 4,000 botany sites are included on this site. You can search by keyword or browse through the alphabetical site list. Another way to browse is by subject including: Arboreta and Botanical Gardens, Gardening and Economic Botany. ∞

**Authority:** Anthony R. Brach, (Harvard University Herbarium, Cambridge / Missouri Botanical Garden) and Raino Lampinen (Botanical Museum, Finnish Museum of Natural History, University of Helsinki)

## KidsGardening!

http://www.kidsgardening.com/

The site says, "Our commitment to support educators and parents has inspired this new website. Our goal is to be the best site for all of you who garden with kids, whether you explore plants and gardens as family projects or as educational tools." To support this grand vision, the National Gardening Association has collected links, articles, activity suggestions, classroom stories, basic plant information and more. Be sure to check out the Parents' Primer. (PreK–Adult)

**Authority:** National Gardening Association

## KinderGARDEN

http://aggie-horticulture.tamu.edu/kindergarden/kinder.htm

"An introduction to the many ways children can interact with plants and the outdoors." The site includes activities, curriculum guides, websites and other information in categories such as Children's Gardens, Fun Page for Kids and Special Tips for Gardening with Kids!

**Authority:** Sarah Lineberger, Dept. of Horticultural Sciences, Texas A&M University

## NeoFlora

http://www.neoflora.com/

"With over 38,000 entries, you'll find everything from trees to tropicals" proclaims the site. It is searchable by common and scientific name. Entries include the scientific name, plant requirements, description and characteristics, plant care tips and pictures. Articles on plant care and problems are also available.

**Authority:** NeoInformatics Inc.

## Plant Fossil Record

http://ibs.uel.ac.uk/palaeo/pfr2/pfr.htm

The "database includes descriptions and occurrences of many thousands of extinct plants. For the first time modern genera with fossil species are included in the description database." The database is divided into the following searchable categories: Genera, Descriptions, Taxonomy, Occurrences and Paleo Maps.

**Authority:** International Organization of Paleobotany

## Plants National Database

http://plants.usda.gov/plantproj/plants/index.html

According to the United States Department of Agriculture, the "PLANTS Database is a single source of standardized information about plants. This database focuses on vascular plants, mosses, liverworts, hornworts and lichens of the U.S. and its territories. The PLANTS Database includes names, checklists, automated tools, identification information, species abstracts, distributional data, crop information, plant symbols, plant growth data, plant materials information, links, references and other plant information. Entries contains brief factual information such as symbol, family, economic importance, growth habit origin, plant synonyms, distribution information with map, wetlands information and references. The site also includes a photo gallery arranged by plant type.

**Authority:** US Dept. of Agriculture, Natural Resources Conservation Service, Biological Conservation Sciences Division, National Plant Data Center

## Virtual Cell

http://www.life.uiuc.edu/plantbio/cell/

This single plant cell can be zoomed in on, cut, turned and manipulated. Each picture includes a brief description of the part of the cell that is being viewed.(Grades 4–12)

**Authority:** Matej Lexa

## WebGarden

http://webgarden.osu.edu/

"WebGarden provides a growing collection of resources for beginning and professional gardeners, students, teachers, professional agronomists and horticulturists," according to the site. There are a multitude of resources including a Plant Dictionary, Internet Links and the Factsheet Database. Ohio State University has collected into the Factsheet database the efforts of 46 other U.S. and Canadian university and government institutions. More than 20,000 pages of Extension fact sheets and bulletins are included in the database. It is searchable by keyword and Boolean expression and can be limited by geographic region.

**Authority:** Dept. of Horticulture and Crop Science, Ohio State University

# Business and Economics (*see also* Career Development; Consumer Information; Patents)

## CEOExpress, Business Links

http://www.ceoexpress.com/

CEO Express is a quick-loading site which indexes hundreds of business information web pages. It is divided into four main sections. 1. Daily News and Info includes business news and journal resources. 2. Business Research includes stock market, financial and company research information. 3. Office Tools & Travel includes reference resources, directories and travel sites. 4. Breaktime includes sports, Dilbert and shopping resources.  ∞

**Authority:** CEOExpress

## Chambers of Commerce Directory

http://clickcity.com/index2.htm

Although most of the chambers are located in the U.S. and Canada, this straightforward directory also contains a searchable database of international Chambers of Commerce. Search by name, city, state or province. Entries include addresses, names, phone numbers, links to e-mail and the Chamber's website, if available.

**Authority:** Click City

## Corporate Information

http://www.corporateinformation.com/

Although more than 350,000 corporate profiles are included in this site's index, Corporate Information goes beyond just providing company information. Company and industry resources for over 30 industries and 100 countries are part of the database and the front page provides links to "breaking news." There are seven main sections here including: Research a company, Research a country's industry, Research by Country, Research Reports, Figure out Company "Extensions," Currency Rates and Research by State.  ∞

**Authority:** Winthrop Corp.

## EconEdLink, CyberTeach

http://econedlink.org/lessons/

This site is a collection of economics lessons for students from kindergarten through high school. It is arranged by title, grade, standard or lesson plan type. Just click any of the headings to re-sort the list.  ✎

**Authority:** National Council on Economic Education

## Economic Resources for K–12 Teachers

http://ecedweb.unomaha.edu/teach.htm

This site organizes its annotated links into the following sections: Curricular Materials, Useful Websites, Web Teaching Ideas, Virtual Economics, Nebraska K–12, Other K–12 Sites, Gopher Sites and EcEdWeb Home.  ∞ ✎

**Authority:** Kim Sosin Co-Director, UNO Center for Economic Education, Chair, Dept. of Economics, College of Business Administration, University of Nebraska at Omaha

## EDGAR

http://www.sec.gov/edgarhp.htm

EDGAR stands for Electronic Data Gathering, Analysis and Retrieval system. This government site makes the required filings—such as annual reports of publicly held companies available online. These reports contain substantial company information such as corporate addresses, balance sheets, gross sales and other financial information.

**Authority:** Securities and Exchange Commission

## FleetKids

http://www.fleetkids.com/

FleetKids is about "encouraging learning through inquiry and getting kids started out on the path to money smarts. It's also about showing kids that money smarts isn't just earning, earning, earning until you're blue in the wallet. Money smarts means working hard, saving and investing. And giving something back to the people who helped you out when you needed it and to people who can reach out and help others." The site contains several games using mathematic, financial and social skills. The games range in title from BuyLo/SellHi to Play Ball! An "Activity Book" located on the first page is a tool to help teachers use the activities on this site. (Grades K–6)

**Authority:** Fleet Kids

## Hoover's Online

http://www.hoovers.com

Information on this site has been divided into two sections. The first part is free and contains company capsules, brief financial information and links to news stories about specific companies. The company capsule includes addresses, telephone numbers, company website links, a brief company description and lists of subsidiaries and competitors. The second part of the site requires a paid membership. More than 13,500 companies are listed in the free database and include both publicly and privately-held companies. The paid-for "profiles" database consists of 3,500+ companies.

**Authority:** Hoover's Inc.

### Industry Research Desk

http://www.virtualpet.com/industry/rdindex2.htm

This is a terrific guide and resource for "researching specific companies, industries and manufacturing processes." It begins with a 14 step guide titled: "How to Learn About an Industry or a Specific Company." The rest of the site sections include: Industry Data, Industry Home Pages, Manufacturing Process Home Pages, North American Industry Classification System (NAICS) to replace Standard Industrial Classification (SIC) codes, Office Tools and Search Engines. Unfortunately, the site contents are not searchable. ∞

**Authority:** Polson Enterprises

### International Business Resources on the Web

http://globaledge.msu.edu/ibrd/ibrd.asp

Created and maintained by the Center for International Business Education and Research at Michigan State University, this site is the leading directory for international business resources on the Internet. It is searchable by keyword. Most of the links are organized into categories such as News/Periodicals, Culture and Language, Government Resources and Trade Tutorials.

**Authority:** Center for International Business Education and Research (MSU-CIBER), Michigan State University

### Investing for Kids

http://library.thinkquest.org/3096/index.htm

"This Website is designed by kids for kids. It examines stocks, bonds, mutual funds and the like. It teaches the principles of saving and investing. It also includes a stock game." The site includes articles such as Concepts of Investing, Types of Investments and Stocks in Cyberspace and other information such as beginner, intermediate and advanced advice, information and resource lists.(Grades 7–Undergraduate)

**Authority:** David Leung, Steven Ngai and Hassan Mirza

### Krislyn's Stricktly Business Sites

http://www.krislyn.com/sites.html

Online since 1995, Krislyn's aim "is to provide a broad list of business sources in a wide variety of areas." Subject areas include Accounting, Management, Business Plans, Sales, Insurance and Manufacturing. The site is searchable by keyword. ∞

**Authority:** Paul J. Wilczynski, Krislyn Corporation

### Lemonade Stand

http://www.littlejason.com/lemonade/

This is a web version of a computer game where the goal is to run a successful lemonade stand. This is a great activity to begin discussion on basic business principles. (Grades 3–6)

**Authority:** Jason C. Mayans

### Money Experience for Kids

http://www.edu4kids.com/money/

Three online games can be played on this site, each one aimed at teaching money skills. The three games are Making Change, Spending Money and Piggy Bank Breaking. There are options for customization of this game including a timer and scoring.(Grades 3–6)

**Authority:** Infobahn Xpress and Tomas Rivera Elementary School, Riverside California

### Salary Calculator

http://www.homefair.com/homefair/cmr/salcalc.html

Compare the cost of living in hundreds of cities in the U.S. and around the world. Choose place of origin and place of destination and proceed through the menus. Results tell you how much money you would need to make in your destination city to maintain your current economic lifestyle.

**Authority:** Homestore.com

### SBA: Hotlist

http://www.sba.gov/hotlist/

The full title of this site is "U.S. Small Business Administration's 3,779 Outside Resources & Great Business Hotlinks." The links are arranged into 38 broad categories such as Starting, Minorities, Franchising and Home Business. The site is keyword-searchable. ∞

**Authority:** U.S. Small Business Administration

### Streetlink Investor Information Center ∞

http://www.streetlink.com/

The site states that it "provides a comprehensive Internet program for public corporations to communicate with shareholders as well as prospective investors. The website allows corporations to display any combination of financial reports, newsworthy items, corporate profiles or annual reports." The information is mounted on this site by the individual companies. While it isn't searchable, it does have a browsable alphabetically linked list.

**Authority:** Streetlink and the individual companies

### Superstar Investor

http://www.superstarinvestor.com/

"Superstar Investor is a guide to the most complete and reliable investment information on the Internet. It highlights the BEST sites, offering clearly written descriptive summaries that serve as a guide to the content within those sites. The level of detail and ease of use make Superstar Investor a unique and valuable financial resource." This website really does live up to its billing, though not all of the links include annotations. The links are categorized into nine sections including: Investor Supersites, Brokerage Firms, Exchanges, Futures & Options, Initial Public Offerings, Mutual Funds, Publications, Quotes & Charts and Research & Analysis. The site does not include a search function. ∞

**Authority:** Superstar Investor

### Thomas Register

http://www.thomasregister.com

Sign up for a free membership to access The Thomas Register. Once you are signed on, the database of manufacturing and industrial companies is available for searching. Search the database by Company Name, Product/Service or Brand Name. Entries include contact information and a brief product description. Web links, clickable e-mail forms and online catalogs are available for some entries. Both U.S. and Canadian companies are included.

**Authority:** Thomas Publishing Company

## Calendars and Holidays (*see also* Reference: Other Virtual Reference Sites)

### Calendar Converter

http://www.fourmilab.to/documents/calendar/

Any date can be converted to Gregorian, Julian, Hebrew, Islamic, Persian, Mayan, Bahai, Indian Civil, French Republican and other computer-based calendars. Each calendar type is accompanied with a paragraph of text describing the system.

**Authority:** John Walker

### Calendar Zone

http://www.calendarzone.com

Calendars of all kinds are categorized into the following: Celestial, Cultural, Daily, Event, Geographic, Historic, Holidays, Interactive, Millennium, Misc., Reference, Reform, Religious, Software, Traditional, Web, Women and Y2K. ∞

**Authority:** Janice McLean

### Diversity Calendar

http://www3.kumc.edu/diversity/

Instead of indexing the Internet this calendar gives brief information about each holiday and occasionally provides links for further clarification about a holiday. The site is arranged into five main areas: Month, Ethnic, National Holiday, Religious and Other. National Holidays refer only to those holidays celebrated in the United States of America.

**Authority:** University of Kansas and the KU Medical Center

### Historic Events and Birth Dates

http://www.scopesys.com/today/

An eclectic collection of "this day in history"-type events that include: Births, Deaths, Reported-Missing in Action, On This Day, Holidays, Religious Observances, Religious History and Thought for the Day. Searchable by day, month and year, not by event. Entries go back in time to at least 1066.

**Authority:** Scope Systems

### Holidays on the Net

http://www.holidays.net/

Select a holiday from the drop down list and you will find a wealth of information. Articles on various decorations or traditions associated with the holiday, a directory to other related websites, a message board and greeting cards are included for every holiday on the list. Some holidays include music and other multimedia pieces. The holiday list is not as comprehensive as other sources, but the information and extras are exceptional. ∞

**Authority:** Studio Melizo

### KIDPROJ's Multi-Cultural Calendar

http://www.kidlink.org/KIDPROJ/MCC/

This wonderful collection of student-written descriptions of holidays and celebrations has contributions from all over the world. This variety ensures that all kinds of holidays are represented in the database, including Bastille Day, Holy Week, Thaipusam and Valentine's Day. The site is keyword-searchable or browsable by month, holiday, country or author.

**Authority:** KIDLINK Society

### Worldwide Holiday & Festival Site

http://www.holidayfestival.com/

Browse through the entries on this site by country or religion. Alternately, use the keyword search function. If the holiday does not fall on a specific date, like Easter, then dates for six years are available.

**Authority:** Brian Prescott-Decie

# Career Development (*see also* Business and Economics; Consumer Information)

## Kids Career Information

http://www.bcit.tec.nj.us/KidCareer/

This learning game is "designed in accordance with the Goals 2000 act, as a means to provide children with an opportunity to learn more about careers available for consideration as they get ready to enter their high school years." The site has several interactive items, including a game and surveys to uncover interests and options. There are links to other career sites.
**Authority:** Burlington County Institute of Technology

## Monster.com

http://www.monster.com/

One of the largest career centers on the Net, Monster.com is divided into three distinct areas. The first, Search Jobs, is a searchable database of hundreds of thousands of jobs. The second, My Monster gets your resume up on the site for prospective employers to view. Finally, Career Center, is the place to get advice and join discussion groups to further your career goals, to find new opportunities and to hone job hunting skills.
**Authority:** Monster.com

## Occupational Outlook Handbook

http://stats.bls.gov/ocohome.htm

Use the keyword search feature to find specific careers or fields of work. Each career page contains the following sections: Nature of the Work, Employment, Job Outlook and Sources of Additional Information. The database contains over 760 occupations.
**Authority:** U.S. Bureau of Labor Statistics

## The Riley Guide

http://www.rileyguide.com

This helpful guide to online job searching includes articles ranging from "how to prepare a resume" to "how to get started." Links to both general job finding sites and industry or occupation specific job sites are available. ∞
**Authority:** Margaret Riley Dikel

## Teenage Jobs, Careers and College

http://www.quintcareers.com/teens.html

This long scroll-down list is organized into three sections: College-Related Resources for Teenagers, Job and Career Resources for Teenagers and Helpful Books for Teenagers. The Job and Career Resources for Teenagers section links to a list of websites aimed at helping teenagers find jobs, internships, job camps and to develop careers. The site links into the larger Quintessential Careers site with its array of career related websites and articles on topics such as how to write cover letters and resumes. ∞
**Authority:** Quintessential Careers

# Chat and Instant Messenger

## AOL Instant Messenger

http://www.aol.com/aim/homenew.adp

This is where you go to download and install AOL Instant Messenger. AOL maintains a directory of Instant Messenger chat rooms at: http://www.aol.com/community/chat/allchats.html
**Authority:** America Online, Inc.

## ICQ

http://web.icq.com/

Download and install the ICQ software from this web page. To find ICQ rooms use the directory at: http://www.icq.com/icqchat/
**Authority:** ICQ Inc.

## MSN Messenger

http://messenger.msn.com/

This is the main address to download MSN's messenger service.
**Authority:** Microsoft Corp.

## Yahoo! Chat

http://chat.yahoo.com/

Sign up and access hundreds of Yahoo! chat rooms from this web page.
**Authority:** Yahoo!

## Yahoo! Messenger

http://messenger.yahoo.com/

Yahoo! Messenger can be downloaded from this site. You can search for people and topics at: http://members.yahoo.com/
**Authority:** Yahoo!

# Chemistry (*see also* Earth Science; Science; Science Fairs)

## BioChemLinks

http://biochemlinks.com/bclinks/bclinks.cfm

BioChemLinks "is a portal to excellent biology, biochemistry and chemistry educational resources." It is arranged into six main sections: General Biology,

General Chemistry organic Chemistry, Biochemistry, Biotechnology and Teaching Science. Under each section is a list of links to other websites that are relevant to the subject. The site is keyword-searchable. (High School–Researcher) ∞

**Authority:** Dyann K. Schmidel, Ph.D.

## Chem Team

http://dbhs.wvusd.k12.ca.us/ChemTeamIndex.html

"The ChemTeam provides study resources in all standard topics for students in high school and Advanced Placement chemistry." The site is arranged by chemical subjects such as acid base, gas laws, equilibrium, thermochemistry and stoichiometry. Each subject contains lengthy articles, problems, exercises and occasional links. (High School–Undergraduate)

**Authority:** John L. Park

## Chem4Kids

http://www.chem4kids.com/

This encyclopedic site has divided its subject matter into five broad categories: Matter, Elements, Atoms, Math and Reactions. Under each category are multiple articles. You may also use the search function to find specific topics. (Grades 3–8)

**Authority:** Kalipi.com and Andrew Rader Studios

## Chemdex.org

http://www.chemdex.org/

Chemdex has indexed chemistry sites on the Web since 1993 and is one of the most comprehensive places to begin searching for chemistry information. It is arranged into the following sections: Universities, Government, Companies, Institutions, Chemistry, Databases, Communication, Software, WWW and Other Links. Chemdex and ChemWeb have teamed up to create a searchable database called ChemDex Plus (available on either site). This database includes almost 6,000 reviewed and annotated chemistry websites. ∞

**Authority:** Dr. Mark J. Winter, Dept. of Chemistry, University of Sheffield

## Chemistry Tutor

http://library.thinkquest.org/2923/

Now part of the ThinkQuest site. This chemistry homework site has grouped information into the following categories: Introduction to Chemistry, Laws & Reactions, Basic Chemistry, Equations & More, Types of Chemical Reactions, Lab Safety, Laboratory Tests to Identify Unknown, Chemistry Calculators, Chemistry/Science Links and Web Elements. Examples, illustrations,

links, articles, charts and graphs are included in each category. (High School–Undergraduate)

**Authority:** Chemistry Tutor

## ChemWeb

http://www.chemweb.com/

ChemWeb is the World Wide Club for the Chemical Community. Use of this site requires signing up for a free membership. It provides access to a Library of leading chemical journals, Databases containing abstracts, chemical structures, patents and websites, *The Alchemist*, ChemWeb's magazine, a Shopping Mall with software, equipment and books, a Worldwide Job Exchange, ACD (Available Chemicals Directory), plus a searchable reviewed database of chemistry resources on the Web. ∞

**Authority:** ChemWeb Inc.

## General Chemistry Online

http://antoine.frostburg.edu/chem/senese/

Everything you wanted to know to pass a general chemistry class is included on this site. There are many subject sections including a glossary, trivia quiz, FAQ, articles and tutorials. There are five invaluable sections: 1. Common Compound Library, "A searchable database of over 800 common compound names, formulas, structures and properties;" 2. Companion Notes, "Hyperlinked notes and guides for first semester general chemistry;" 3. Resources, "A searchable, annotated database of over 400 general chemistry web resources;" 4. Toolbox, "Interactive graphing, popup tables and calculators;" 5. Tutorials, "Index of self-guided tutorials, quizzes and drills on specific topics." The site includes a keyword search option. (High School–Undergraduate)

**Authority:** Fred Senese

## WebElements

http://www.webelements.com

This site accesses a periodic table with comprehensive descriptions, pictures and information about the elements.

**Authority:** Dr. Mark J. Winter, Dept. of Chemistry, University of Sheffield

# Codes

## Codes, Ciphers, & Codebreaking

http://vectorsite.tripod.com/ttcode0.html

The site states that "Codes and codebreaking [have] been politically and militarily important for most of recorded history. They have been the products of brilliant ingenuity and with modern computer networking have become important in day-to-day life. This document provides a technical and historical survey of the techniques of making and breaking codes."

**Authority:** Greg Goebel

### Codes, Ciphers and Secret Messages

http://eduscapes.com/42explore/codes.htm

Part of the larger eduScapes website. This page discusses the basics of secret codes and links to many other related sites. The links cover topics such as Morse Code, Decoding Nazi Secrets and Data Encryption. ∞

**Authority:** Annette Lamb and Larry Johnson

### Morse Code Translator

http://www.bsa.scouting.org/nav/scouts.html

Put a word to be translated into Morse code in the first box. Use the second box to change Morse code into a word or phrase. There is also a page called, "Say It With Semaphores." The use of flag positions as communication is called "semaphore code." Put a word in the search box to get the semaphore positions. Alternately click on either easy or hard and get a semaphore to test your reading ability. The site is currently using frames, so click on "Family Fun" to get to the Morse Code Translator and Semaphores links.

**Authority:** Boy Scouts of America

# Consumer Information (*see also* Business and Economics; Currency Converters)

### Consumer Information Center

http://www.pueblo.gsa.gov/

The well-known Consumer Information Center in Pueblo, Colorado authors this site. It contains full-text versions of the consumer pamphlets put out by the federal government. The following information categories are included: Cars, Children, Education, Employment, Federal Programs, Food, Health, Housing, Money, Small Business, Travel and more..., Consumer Help, Contact Center, Kids.Gov, Recalls and Scams/Frauds.

**Authority:** U.S. Consumer Information Center, General Services Administration

### Consumer Product Safety Commission

http://www.cpsc.gov/

The U.S. Consumer Product Safety Commission is an independent federal regulatory agency that was "created in 1972 by Congress in the Consumer Product Safety Act. In that law, Congress directed the Commission to: protect the public against unreasonable

risks of injuries and deaths associated with consumer products." They have "jurisdiction over about 15,000 types of consumer products, from automatic-drip coffee makers to toys to lawn mowers." Information on this site is organized under the headings: Business, Consumer/Espanol, 4 Kids, Library/FOIA, Press Room, Recalls/News and Report Unsafe Products.

**Authority:** United States Consumer Product Safety Commission

### Consumer Search

http://www.consumersearch.com/www/

"Reviewing the Reviewers" is the slogan for this extraordinary site. They rank, describe and analyze the product reviews of all of the top reviewers. *PC World*, *The Wall Street Journal* and Yahoo! Internet Life have all given top reviews of this site. There are reviews and links for everything from computers to exercise equipment.

**Authority:** ConsumerSearch Inc.

### Consumer World

http://www.consumerworld.org/

Over 2,000 consumer resources are categorized here. To find information use the keyword search feature or the site directory with the broad categories like: News, Agencies, Resources, Companies, Travel, Money, Bargains, Shopping and Internet. ∞

**Authority:** Edgar Dworsky

### CNET.com

http://www.cnet.com/

There are extensive reviews and buying guides for all things electronic on this site. "The company's vision is to educate and empower people and businesses by unlocking the potential of the technology world to make things easier and faster and by helping them make smarter buying decisions." This is definitely the place to start when trying to make up your mind about computer hardware or software.

**Authority:** CNET Networks, Inc.

### Directory of Better Business Bureaus

http://www.bbb.org/

Find a BBB by searching via zip code, clicking on a state listing or clicking on the image map of the United States. Each subsequent page has addresses, phone numbers and other contact information. You can also Check out a Company, File a Complaint, read up-to-date Consumer Information or Check out a Charity.

**Authority:** Council of Better Business Bureaus

## Edmunds.com

http://www.edmunds.com

One of the major U.S. car buying guides, Edmunds has resources for appraising, buying, selling and evaluating both new and used cars. Click either New or Used to begin surfing through the reviews or try one of the other categories such as Reviews, Advice, News, Ownership and Town Hall.

Authority: Edmunds.com

## Epinions.com

http://www.epinions.com/

Have an opinion on something? Want to find what regular people think of a product or service? Then visit this site and browse through hundreds of reviews organized by category: Arts & Entertainment, Autos & Motorsports, Business & Technology, Computers & Internet, Electronics, Home & Garden, Hotels & Travel, Kids & Family, Personal Finance, Restaurants & Gourmet, Sports & Outdoors and Wellness & Beauty.

Authority: Epinions Inc.

## Kelley Blue Book Used Car Guide

http://www.kbb.com/

Probably the best-known of the U.S. car buying guides, the Blue Book has lots of useful information on buying, selling and evaluating new and used cars and motorcycles. The site also has a "Lemon Check" service to learn about a specific car's history.

Authority: Kelley Blue Book

## MMI Educational Resources

http://www.moneymanagement.org/Education/Resources/

Scroll down the page to access the list of lesson plans designed to "provide educators with strategies for teaching personal finance education in the classroom." Each lesson plan listed in this section includes a lesson description, a personal finance concepts list, cross-curricular connections, instructional objectives, detailed procedure steps, activity sheets and visuals, assessment techniques and extension/enrichment recommendations. (Grades 3–6)

Authority: Money Management International

## NADA Guides

http://www.nadaguides.com

N.A.D.A. "works independent of any third party special interest groups to arrive at the most accurate, reliable and unbiased vehicle values in the industry." The site has information on New Cars, Used Cars, Classic Cars, Power Sports, Marine, Recreation Vehicles, Aircraft and Manufactured Housing.

Authority: N.A.D.A. Appraisal Guides Inc.

## National Consumer Law Center

http://www.consumerlaw.org/

Don't get sidetracked by all of the material available for purchase. The useful part of the site is farther down the first page under the heading Free Consumer Information. Extensive articles written by the National Consumer Law Center are grouped under the following categories: Protecting Your Home, Protecting Yourself, What You Need to Know About Credit Reports, Utility Service Tips and Unfair Sales Practices to Avoid.

Authority: National Consumer Law Center

## What's a Dollar Worth?

http://woodrow.mpls.frb.fed.us/economy/calc/cpihome.html

"The Consumer Price Index (CPI) is the ratio of the value of a basket of goods in the current year to the value of that same basket of goods in an earlier year. It measures the average level of prices of the goods and services typically consumed by an urban American family. Parkin, 1990" This site can calculate the Consumer Price Index based on dollars. The years span 1913–2001.

Authority: Rob Grunewald

# Copyright

## Copyright Clearance Center

http://www.copyright.com/

"Copyright Clearance Center, Inc., the largest licensor of text reproduction rights in the world, was formed in 1978 to facilitate compliance with U.S. copyright law." According to the site you can "get permission to reproduce copyrighted content such as articles and book chapters in your journals, photocopies, coursepacks, library reserves, websites, e-mail and more." Click on the large graphic to access "Permissions Online."

Authority: Copyright Clearance Center, Inc.

## Copyright Resources on the Internet

http://groton.k12.ct.us/mts/pt2a.htm

This is a great directory of copyright resources. It is organized into chapters including Fair Use Guidelines, Citing Sources and Copyright Resources K–12.

Authority: Steve Smith, Media Technology Services

## Copyright Website

http://www.copyrightwebsite.com/

"This portal provides real world, practical and relevant copyright information for anyone navigating the net." It is organized into five tabs: Wizard, Visual, Audio, Digital and Info. Within the five tabs are articles, issues, cases, software and other copyright resources and information.

Authority: Benedict O'Mahoney, Copyright Website

## U.S. Copyright Office

http://www.loc.gov/copyright/

This site "has been created with the desire to serve the copyright community of creators and users, as well as the general public. Here you will find all our key publications, including informational circulars; application forms for copyright registration; links to the copyright law and to the homepages of other copyright-related organizations; news of what the Office is doing, including Congressional testimony and press releases; our latest regulations; a link to our online copyright records cataloged since 1978 and much more." The site is divided into the following sections: What's New, General Information, Publications, Copyright Office Records, Legislation, Announcements, International and Copyright Links.

Authority: U.S. Copyright Office

# Currency Converters

## Oanda Currency Converter and Financial Forecasts

http://www.oanda.com/

This site converts more than 164 currencies from around the world. There is also an easy-to-use quick conversion for the 18 most commonly used currencies. The information is updated daily at 8:00 p.m. Eastern Standard Time.

Authority: OANDA

## The Universal Currency Converter

http://www.xe.net/currency/

This currency converter has two parts. The first is smaller and indexes the 90 most commonly used currencies. The second part builds on the first part for a grand total of 180 currencies. Over 250 countries are represented in the database.

Authority: Xenon Laboratories

# Dance (*see also* Drama; Music; Prizes and Awards)

## American Ballroom Companion: Dance Instruction Manuals ca.1490–1920

http://lcweb2.loc.gov/ammem/dihtml/dihome.html

Part of the American Memory Project, the "American Ballroom Companion presents a collection of more than two hundred social dance manuals at the Library of Congress." There is a Video Directory indexing 75 video clips that "illustrate portions of the Dance Instruction Manuals." The clips are in various web media types such as QuickTime and MPEG. The site is searchable by keyword and browsable by author, subject and title.

Authority: U.S. Library of Congress

## Artlynx International Dance Resources

http://www.artslynx.org/dance/

Artlynx attempts "to allow users to easily navigate to the many amazing dance link libraries available online, but where we find gaps, Artlynx aims to fill them with its own original set of dance and ballet resources." The scope of this site is quite breathtaking with links and information arranged into the categories such as: Original Artlynx Materials, Master Sites, Dancer Health & Safety Resources and Ethnic Dance Resources. ∞

Authority: Richard Finkelstein, Editor

## CyberDance Ballet on the Net

http://www.cyberdance.org/

"This is a collection of over 3,500 links to classical ballet and modern dance resources on the Internet." It is organized by broad subject category such as Schools, Summer Programs and Dance Websites. The database is searchable by keyword. ∞

Authority: Rose Ann Willenbrink and CyberDance

## Dance Directory

http://www.sapphireswan.com/dance/

"The goal of the Sapphire Swan Dance Directory is to provide links to the best dance resources available on the Web." The database provides links to "three kinds of dance websites: 1. sites that have good collections of links, usually in a specialized area of dance, 2. sites that include information about an area of dance and 3. selected sites of dance organizations and individual dancers." To access the data, use the list of dance styles on the left side menu bar. ∞

Authority: Sapphire Swan

### New York Public Library Dance Collection

http://www.nypl.org/research/lpa/dan/dan.html

New York Public has one of the most extensive collections of dance resources in the United States. This page offers instruction and access points to many dance resources including the "Selected Dance Resources on the Internet" list. NYPL has created an online version of the New York Catalog of the Dance Collection, a staple of most reference collections. To access the catalog go to http://catnyp.nypl.org and scroll down to the link titled "Connect to the DANCE COLLECTION CATALOG."

**Authority:** New York Public Library

# Dictionaries (*see also* Grammar; Writing and Style Guides; Reference: Other Virtual Reference Sites; Thesauri)

### Dictionary.com

http://www.dictionary.com/

The "Look Up" box searches many well known dictionaries such as Webster's and The American Heritage. Each search results in a list of definitions from the various dictionaries. This is probably the simplest dictionary to use on the Internet.

**Authority:** Lexico LLC

### Little Explorers Picture Dictionary

http://www.LittleExplorers.com/

More than just a picture dictionary, this site uses the pictures as a place to start browsing the Internet. More than 600 sites are linked to the pictures. Each site has been chosen because it is "appropriate, enjoyable, educational and interesting." There is a lot of "help" information on this site with recommended classroom activities and an educators guide. (Grades PreK–3)

**Authority:** Enchanted Learning Software

### OneLook Dictionaries

http://www.onelook.com/

OneLook is a dictionary search system that searches more than 700 online dictionaries. There is a browsable list of links to those dictionaries. This site can search for definitions of slang terms and can return definitions in other languages such as Chinese.

**Authority:** OneLook

### Terminology Collection Online Dictionaries

http://www.uwasa.fi/comm/termino/collect

The home page has two pulldown selections. The first is Word-Online, which contains links to foreign language dictionaries. The second is Term-Online, which contains links to subject specific dictionaries. There are also links for acronyms, fun and slang dictionaries.

**Authority:** Anita Nuopponen, Dept. of Communication Studies, University of Vaasa, Finland

### Word2Word

http://www.word2word.com/

This extensive site is a collection of links that index language resource sites on the Web. All kinds of resources are here including language chat sites, translating services, language courses and a multitude of dictionaries and translators. Just click on Online Dictionaries and Translators and the "Take Me To" button and you will access the chart of language dictionaries that include everything from Klingon to German. ∞

**Authority:** Word2Word

### Your Dictionary.Com

http://www.yourdictionary.com

Over 800 dictionaries and 150 languages are represented in this collection. Languages include Afrikaans, Latvian, Manx, Sranan, Welsh and Yiddish among others. A list of language related resources is also available.

**Authority:** Robert Beard, Linguistics Dept., Bucknell University

# Drama (*see also* Art; Music; Prizes and Awards)

### Acting Workshop On-Line

http://www.redbirdstudio.com/AWOL/acting2.html

This is for aspiring actors and includes many articles and resources. Below all the introductory material on the initial page is a list of lessons created by A.W.O.L. Each lesson is several pages in length and includes examples and instructions. Lessons range from Help! I Gotta Get a Monolog!!! to How To Audition for a Musical.

**Authority:** Acting Workshop On Line

### Creative Drama and Theatre Education Resources Site

http://www.creativedrama.com/

This drama page is divided into the following sections: Creative Drama, Classroom Ideas, Theatre Games, Plays for Performance, Book List, Search, Discussion, Feedback and About the Author. Each category contains relevant information created or compiled by the site author. For instance, the Creative Drama section links to a lengthy essay and the Theatre Games lists drama activities with explanations and instructions. The page has not been updated since 1999. However, the links are still functional and the content is useful. Hopefully, the page will be updated in the near future. (Grades K–12) ✎

**Authority:** Janine Moyer-Buesgen

### Drama Teacher's Resource Room

http://www3.sk.sympatico.ca/erachi/

This page is arranged into four major sections: Lesson Plans, Backstage, Texts and Seminars and Great Drama Links. Each lesson plan comes with suggested grade levels. Articles ranging from props to lighting can be found under Backstage. The Great Drama Links page includes resources for "classroom or production work." (Grades K–12) ✎

**Authority:** Thornton Consulting & Training Services

### Mr. William Shakespeare and the Internet

http://shakespeare.palomar.edu/

Two objectives guide the development of this site. The first is "to be a complete annotated guide to the scholarly Shakespeare resources available on Internet" and the second is "to present new Shakespeare material unavailable elsewhere on the Internet." Content unique to this site includes the following items: The Shakespeare Timeline, A Shakespeare Genealogy, A Shakespeare Timeline Summary Chart, A Shakespeare Biography Quiz, The Shakespeare Canon, Charles and Mary Lamb's Tales From Shakespeare and more. The site is searchable.

**Authority:** Terry A. Gray, Palomar College

### Performing Arts Links

http://www.theatrelibrary.org/links/

This site indexes performing arts websites into the following categories: Organizations; Museums & Collections; University Departments and Libraries, Theatre Schools; Cinema; Dance; Theatre; Reviews; and Libraries: General Resources. The categories include international links. ⊘

**Authority:** Maria Teresa Lovinelli, Vice Director, Burcardo Library and Theatre Collection.

### Theatre History Websites

http://www.win.net/~kudzu/history.html

This page is a lengthy list of websites arranged into the following broad categories: General Information, Classical Theatre Websites, Medieval Theatre, Elizabethan Theatre, Later English Theatre (Including the former Empire), The Illusionistic Stage, American Theatre and

Other Theatre Links. It may not have a search engine, but it is very up-to-date and quite comprehensive. ⊘

**Authority:** Jerry Bangham, Associate Professor of Speech and Theatre, Alcorn State University

### Theatre Link

http://www.theatre-link.com/

This useful site is a directory of hundreds of websites related to the Theatre. It is searchable by keyword or browsable by categories such as Goods and Services, Shows and Performances, Shakespeare and Academic Programs. ⊘

**Authority:** Scott Naef

# Earth Science (*see also* Geology; Science; Weather and Climate)

### Athena, Earth and Space Science for K–12

http://www.athena.ivv.nasa.gov/

An interesting array of earth and space science instructional materials are integrated into this one site. It is divided into seven sections: Space, Weather, Earth, Oceans, & More, For Teachers and What's New. Each section includes article length information, activities and links to other resources. (Grades K–12)

**Authority:** Dr. Hugh Anderson, Science Applications International Corporation (SAIC)

### Destination Earth

http://www.earth.nasa.gov/

"NASA's Earth Science Enterprise is dedicated to understanding the total Earth system and the effects of humans on the global environment." There is a great deal of information provided on this site. Of primary interest is the "For Kids Only" section which contains multimedia essays, games and activities. Another relevant section is "Teaching Earth Science" section which includes educational materials, reports, product reviews and links. Other sections on this site include Earth Science Enterprise Studio and Breaking News. (Grades 3–Undergraduate)

**Authority:** Sharon Sample, SAIC Information Services, NASA

### Earth Science Resources

http://sln.fi.edu/tfi/hotlists/geology.html

The Franklin Institute has created a directory to many educational earth science resources. The sites range in topic from Volcanos to Aquatic Ecosystems. ⊘

**Authority:** Franklin Institute

## Earth Systems

http://www.cotf.edu/ete/modules/msese/earthsys.html

This user-friendly site is arranged into the following categories: Diversity, Adaptation, Plate Tectonics, Cycles, Spheres, Biomes and Geologic Time. Each of these categories lead to informative articles, illustrations, charts and links. (Grades 5–8)

**Authority:** Dr. Robert Myers, Wheeling Jesuit University/NASA Classroom of the Future

## Earthforce

http://www.fi.edu/earth/earth.html

"If you have ever felt the rumble of an earthquake or seen the eruption of a volcano, you've witnessed EARTHFORCE." This site provides information about the various forces at work on/in the earth, including Volcanoes, Earthquakes, Floods, Tsunami and Avalanches. Each section consists of an essay with embedded links to other related sites. ∞

**Authority:** Franklin Institute Science Museum

## Exploring Planets in the Classroom

http://www.soest.hawaii.edu/SPACEGRANT/class_acts/

Begin exploring the planets in our solar system with this site. It starts out with the following table of contents: Introduction to Solar System, Planetary Properties, Volcanology, Impact Craters, Dynamic Earth, Gradation, Gravity Forces & Rockets, The Moon and Remote Sensing. This site has over 25 hands on activities for "teachers and students for exploring Earth, the planets, geology and space sciences." A short list of related websites are included. (Grades K–12)

**Authority:** Linda Martel, Curator and the Hawaii Space Grant Consortium

## Glacier

http://www.glacier.rice.edu/

This is "a website all about Antarctica and the part Antarctica plays in our global system of weather and climate and oceans and geology!" The main categories on this information rich site are Introduction, Weather, Expedition, Ice, Global Connections and Oceans. Each of these sections is subdivided by topic and includes a glossary, bibliography and additional links. (Grades 9–Undergraduate)

**Authority:** Rice University, West Antarctic Ice Sheet Initiative, Education Development Center of Massachusetts, educators from Texas, Colorado, Massachusetts and Maine and Teachers Experiencing Antarctica (TEA) participants

## Ocean Planet

http://seawifs.gsfc.nasa.gov/OCEAN_PLANET/HTML/ocean_planet_overview.html

This complex and detailed site was produced by the Smithsonian Institution as an extension of an exhibit. The exhibit map is used as a navigational tool for the website. Click on any of the rooms to find exhibit images and descriptive information. The map shows the following rooms: Theater, Immersion, Ocean Science, Sea People, Sea Store, Oceans in Peril, Heroes, Reflections, Resources and Museum Shop. You can also search for images or objects by keyword or browse through a subject list. (Grades K–Undergraduate)

**Authority:** Smithsonian Institution

## Powers of Nature

http://www.germantown.k12.il.us/html/title.html

Two categories of powers of nature are included on this site: Meteorological and Geological. Under each category is a list of topics which lead to extensive articles with embedded hypertext links to other related information. Topics found under the geological category include: Slope Failure, Earthquake, Tsunami and Volcano. Topics found under the meteorological category include: Drought, Flood, Hurricane, Blizzard, Tornado and Wildfire. (Grades K–12)

**Authority:** Germantown Elementary School

## Rainbows

http://www.unidata.ucar.edu/staff/blynds/rnbw.html

This essay on rainbows includes hypertext links to related information. For instance, the paragraph about rainbows and refracted light links to an article about light refraction. Other information on this page includes experiments, references and links to other sites. (Grades K–12)

**Authority:** Beverly T. Lynds

# E-Books (*see also* Full Text Resources)

## Can E-Books Improve Libraries?

http://skyways.lib.ks.us/central/ebooks/

Created for a preconference, this site includes practically everything you ever wanted to know about e-books. There are sections on technology, usability, readability, accessibility, awards and review sources.

**Authority:** Chris Rippel, Central Kansas Library System

## eBooks.com

http://www.ebooks.com/

eBooks.com is a commercial retailer of full-text electronic books. Unlike netLibrary which partners with libraries to bring electronic books to individuals, eBooks sells titles directly to the individual.

**Authority:** eBooks.com

## netLibrary

http://www.netlibrary.com/

netLibrary is a service libraries can purchase to provide full-text access to books via the Internet to their patrons. Although the site does include more than 40,000 e-books that are in the public domain, the requirement to log on with a paid subscription limits the usefulness of this site. However, a paid subscription opens up an amazing number of full-text searchable books to your community.

**Authority:** netLibrary Inc.

## PLA Tech Note: E-Books

http://www.pla.org/technotes/ebooks.html

The Public Library Association has written a brief guide to electronic books. The text includes embedded links to other resources and a great bibliography for further research. A definite "must read" if you are not familiar with what e-books are and the issues surrounding them.

**Authority:** GraceAnne A. DeCandido, Public Library Association

# Education: Directories

## American School Directory

http://www.asd.com/

More than 108,000 K–12 U.S. school sites are included in this database. Search by school name or state.

**Authority:** American School Directory

## Education Resource Organizations Directory

http://www.ed.gov/Programs/EROD/

Created by the United States Department of Education, this directory indexes more than 4,000 organizations. Organizations such as Comprehensive Regional Assistance Centers and State Arts Agencies are included. "The Directory is intended to help you identify and contact organizations that provide information and assistance on a broad range of education-related topics." The site is well organized and has a great search engine.

**Authority:** U.S. Dept. of Education

## National Public School Locator

http://nces.ed.gov/ccdweb/school/

This tool produced by the U.S. government searches for public elementary, middle and secondary schools. There are many ways to search including name, area code, school characteristics and location. The results screen will list matching schools with their addresses and phone numbers. Click on a specific school to get statistical data. There is a link toward the bottom of the page that goes to a directory of private schools.

**Authority:** U.S. Dept. of Education

## Peter Milbury's School Librarian Web Pages

http://www.school-libraries.net/

The goal for this site is to index websites that have been created by school librarians. The site is organized by country and state then by School Libraries, K–12 Schools, Curriculum Related Resources, Professional Associations and Personal & Other Types. ∞

**Authority:** Peter Milbury, School Librarian, Chico Senior High School

## Scholarly Societies Project

http://www.scholarly-societies.org

This directory includes over 2,300 Scholarly Societies. The database is searchable by keyword, abbreviation, founding year, geographical area, languages or society name. The site is browsable via the alphabetically arranged subject guides or other categories.

**Authority:** Scholarly Societies Project

## School Libraries on the Web

http://www.sldirectory.com

"This is a list of library web pages maintained by K–12 school libraries in the United States and in countries around the world. This directory is limited to listing pages which focus on the school library/media center." First select a country then choose from the alphabetic list of links. For the United States choose the state then the school library/media center. A search engine on the site is keyword-searchable.

**Authority:** Linda Bertland, Librarian, Stetson Middle School, Philadelphia, Pennsylvania

# Education: Teacher and Student Resources

## A to Z Home's Cool Homeschooling

http://www.gomilpitas.com/homeschooling/

This site contains "over 700 pages of the best and most interesting and useful sites and articles about home education on the Web." The pages are divided into subject categories including: Just Beginning, Concerns about Homeschooling, Study Materials and Lessons & Ideas. Relevant links can also be found by keyword searching or browsing through the alphabetical title list. The site also contains a list of new Home Schooling books. (Grades K–12)

**Authority:** Ann Zeise

## Awesome Library

http://www.awesomelibrary.org/

In selecting resources for this site, EDI has used three main objectives: "1. Programs and studies to promote long term world peace; 2. Programs to enhance communication through the use of web-based solutions; and 3. Studies to evaluate solutions in the fields of health, education and criminal justice." The site "contains 16,000 carefully reviewed resources." Use this site by searching via keyword or by selecting a user category: Teachers, Kids, Teens, Parents, Librarians and Community. From the user category page you can select from various charts to access the website lists. Some of the chart headings include: Subjects, Activities, Fun, Support and Resources.

**Authority:** EDI and Dr. R. Jerry Adams

## B.J. Pinchbeck's Homework Helper

http://school.discovery.com/homeworkhelp/ bjpinchbeck/

This kid friendly site states that it has "more than 700 terrific links to educational sites on the Internet that we think you'll really like." The site is organized alphabetically by subject discipline such as art and science.

**Authority:** Bruce B. Pinchbeck and B.J. Pinchbeck, Discovery.com

## Blue Web'n Learning Applications Library

http://www.kn.pacbell.com/wired/bluewebn/

The selection process for inclusion in this site is fairly demanding. A site must fit the following three criteria: 1. Format must be user-friendly, aesthetically courteous and aesthetically appealing; 2. Content must be credible, useful, rich and interdisciplinary; 3. Learning Process must include higher-order thinking, be engaging and include multiple intelligence or talents. The front page is divided into three headings: Browse the Content Table, Search by Subject Area and Refined Search by Grade Level. The subject area browse uses the Dewey Decimal system to categorize the database. The content table lists first the broad subject group then the types of resources that are available. Resource

types include tutorials, activities, projects, lessons, hot lists, resources and references/tools.

**Authority:** Pacific Bell

## Collaborative Lesson Archive

http://faldo.atmos.uiuc.edu/CLA/index.html

Lesson plans are arranged first by grade level, beginning with preschool and ending with undergraduate. Each grade level is organized into subject area, with lesson plans listed. This site is very interactive with lesson plans being posted by individuals and commentary about lesson plans being posted. The site is searchable by subject, title, grade level and keyword. (Grades K–Undergraduate)

**Authority:** Individual Teachers

## Ed Helper

http://www.edhelper.com/

This is a very large site boasting more than 10,000 Lesson Plans, 1,200+ WebQuests, 600+ File Downloads, 8,500+ Additional Educational Sites, 4,000 Free Worksheet Generators, 1000+ Word and Critical Thinking Problems, Exams and Puzzles for Standardized Tests and Educational News. It is organized into subject categories and includes a discussion board. (Grades K–12)

**Authority:** edHelper.com.

## Education World

http://www.education-world.com/

More than 500,000 education websites, lesson plans, curriculum, guides and other resources are represented in this enormous database. It is searchable or browsable via the subject directory. The site features news articles and "cool sites" every week.

**Authority:** Education World

## Educational Index

http://www.educationindex.com/

Education related sites are reviewed, annotated and dropped into two lists. The first is arranged by subject and the second by education level or what they call "lifestage." A keyword search option is not available at this time.

**Authority:** College View Partners

## FREE: Federal Resources for Educational Excellence

http://www.ed.gov/free/

"Hundreds of education resources supported by agencies across the U.S. Federal government are now easier to find." The resources are arranged by broad subject headings including: Arts, Educational technology, Foreign languages, Health and Safety, Language arts, Mathematics, Physical education, Science, Social studies and Vocational education. ∞

**Authority:** U.S. Dept. of Education

## HighSchool Hub

http://highschoolhub.org/hub/hub.cfm

"The High School Hub is a noncommercial portal to excellent free online academic resources for high school students." The site is divided into sections such as Subject Guides, Updated Daily, Learning Activities and Reference Collection. Within the sections are activities, an ongoing teen poetry contest and links to hundreds of free resources (Grades 9–12) ∞

**Authority:** Dyann K. Schmidel & Wanda G. Wojcik

## Jiskha Homework Help

http://www.jiskha.com/

This homework help website offers assistance with: Art, Computers, English, Foreign Languages, Health, Home Economics, Mathematics, Music, Physical Education, Science, Social Studies and Technology. There are articles written for this site and links to articles on other sites. ∞

**Authority:** Jiskha Productions

## Kathy Schrock's Guide for Educators

http://school.discovery.com/schrockguide/

Now sponsored by the Discovery Channel, this site is one that has been providing great access to educational information on the Net since 1995. According to the site, it is a "categorized list of sites on the Internet found to be useful for enhancing curriculum and teacher professional growth." This site is arranged by subject. It is probably one of the most up-to-date education topic directories on the net. ∞ ✒

**Authority:** Kathleen B. Schrock, MLS

## Kid Info

http://www.kidinfo.com/

This site has been divided into four distinct areas: Student Index, Teacher Index, Parent Index and Young Children. Each of these areas list links to other websites including those that are indexes themselves and are further subdivided by curricular subject area. This site checks its links and updates its content on a weekly basis. The designers have made obvious and effective efforts to include only quality sites. ∞

**Authority:** Linda Guterba

## KidsClick!

http://sunsite.berkeley.edu/KidsClick!/

You can search by subject, browse the subjects alphabetically or use the broad categories on the front page to drill down through this wonderful site. Each subject page includes a list of annotated links that have been selected for inclusion by librarians. Annotations include notes for reading level and number of illustrations. The site has more than 6,500 links. (Grades K–7) ∞

**Authority:** Librarians at the Ramapo Catskill Library System

## Lesson Plans & Reproducibles

http://teacher.scholastic.com/lessonrepro/index.asp

The well-known publisher Scholastic Inc. created this site to facilitate the exchange of lesson plans, ideas and reproducibles. Search for entries based on grade level and discipline such as language arts, science, social science or math. There is a special area for Internet Field Trips. (Grades PreK–8)

**Authority:** Scholastic Inc.

## StudyWeb

http://www.studyweb.com/

Over "162,000 Research Quality URLs" are categorized and reviewed on this vast site. It is searchable by keyword or browsable via any of the following subject categories such as Agriculture, Animals & Pets, Communications, Grammar & Composition, Social Studies & Culture and Other Resources. ∞

**Authority:** Lightspan Inc.

## Teachers Network

http://www.teachnet.org/docs.cfm

This site consists of "teacher designed projects and activities." To find resources select a subject such as English/Language, Instructional Inquiry, Science or Social Science and a grade level from the drop down lists then click on the search button. ✒

**Authority:** Teachers Network, Inc.

## Theme-Related Resources on the World Wide Web

http://www.stemnet.nf.ca/CITE/

The Gander Academy has arranged hundreds of websites by subject category such as Origami, Vikings and Environment. Click on "Teaching With Technology" to get to another subject list of websites. This list includes topics such as Educational Listservs, Software Reviews and Multimedia. ∞

**Authority:** Centre for Innovative Technology in Education

# Educational Television

### A&E

http://www.aande.com/

Click on Classroom from the top menu bar, then scroll down the page to access the following sections: Resources, Study Guides, Communication and Cable Modem Features. Classroom materials, calendars, suggestions and links can be found on this page. The goal of this site is "to help teachers plan classroom discussions and research projects based on A&E's shows." A free educator's guide is available.

**Authority:** Arts & Entertainment Television Network.

### C-SPAN

http://www.c-span.org/

Lesson plans and activity materials on this page relate to C-SPAN television programs. Click on Classroom from the top menu bar to enter the education section of this site. Scroll down the page to find the links to the Teacher Guides/Materials.

**Authority:** National Cable Satellite Corp.

### Cable in the Classroom

http://www.ciconline.com/

CiC Online is provided to help educators make use of no-charge, nonviolent, commercial-free, educational programming. Browse through the subject categories or go to advanced search to use keyword searching. A Long range planner, support materials for specific programs and taping calendars are just a few of the valuable features.

**Authority:** CCI/Crosby Publishing & Cable in the Classroom

### Discovery Channel School

http://school.discovery.com/

The three sections on this site are: For Students featuring homework help, For Teachers with curriculum resources and For Parents with ideas for helping children succeed. There are tons of lesson plans, multimedia games, sound and movies relating to various shows on the Discovery Channel.

**Authority:** Discovery Communications Inc.

### History Channel

http://www.historychannel.com/

Click on "classroom" from the top menu bar to access the classroom calendar, study guides, links, Ideas from our Teachers, This Week in History and the search engine. There are more than 200 study guides for all kinds of history topics.

**Authority:** Arts & Entertainment Television Networks

### The Learning Channel

http://tlc.discovery.com/

The Learning Channel is owned by Discover Communications (Discovery Channel) and much of its content can be searched from that site: http://school.discovery.com. This site includes television schedules and brief descriptions of the programs, but not a lot for teaching at this time. A search button allows you to execute keyword searches either on an individual channel or on all of the following simultaneously: Learning Channel, Discovery Channel, Discovery Health, Travel Channel and Animal Planet.

**Authority:** Discovery Communications Inc.

### PBS Online

http://www.pbs.org/

Explore the website by subject using the drop down subject menu, browse through the Programs A–Z or the TV Schedules or search by keyword. Within the subject areas are lesson plans, video clips, calendars, activities and stories related to the programs featured on PBS. The downside of this site is that when the television program is no longer being played on PBS the resources relating to the program are removed. The site includes programming schedules and a directory to find your local PBS station.

**Authority:** PBS Online

# Encyclopedias (see also Reference: Other Virtual Reference Sites)

### Britannica.com

http://www.britannica.com/

Produced by the makers of the Encyclopedia Brittanica and redesigned in 2001, this incredible site offers a mix of articles from the encyclopedia, websites, magazines, a dictionary and a thesaurus. Use the search box in the middle of the page to do a keyword search. You can also select the section of the index you wish to restrict the search to, such as thesaurus or encyclopedia. ∞

**Authority:** Encyclopedia Britannica, Inc. and Britannica.com Inc.

### Columbia Encyclopedia

http://www.bartleby.com/65/

The complete contents of the sixth edition of this single volume print encyclopedia are found here. "Containing nearly 51,000 entries" and "more than 80,000 hypertext cross-references" the encyclopedia is a good place to start finding answers on a wide variety of topics. Search by keyword or browse alphabetically for the articles.

**Authority:** Columbia University Press

### Encyclopedia Smithsonian

http://www.si.edu/resource/faq/start.htm

This quality site "features answers to frequently asked questions about the Smithsonian and links to Smithsonian resources from A to Z. Browse through the alphabetic list to find relevant links." The Smithsonian has a staggering array of resources on topics from pandas to space flight.

**Authority:** Smithsonian Institution

### Encyclopdia.com

http://www.encyclopedia.com/

The entries on this site are short, "so you can check facts fast. But you can also pursue a train of thought through our extensive cross-references." There are links to related websites and books—"along with links to millions of articles and pictures from the Electric Library (a leading premium research service on the Internet)." To find information, use the search box or browse the alphabetically arranged encyclopedia articles. Over 50,000 articles from the 6th edition of the Concise Columbia Electronic Encyclopedia are included in this online service. Results screens include a short essay with links embedded in the text to related articles.

**Authority:** Infonautics Corporation

### Why Files

http://www.whyfiles.org

This is science information in a kid-friendly format. Use the search feature or click on "Archives" to access the Why Files by the following categories: Biology, Earth & Space Science, Environment, Health, Physical Science, Social Science, Technology. Each Why File entry contains images, links and is usually quite lengthy as it explores each topic in depth. Topics include amber, mars rock, mad cow disease, love and chicken genetics.

**Authority:** University of Wisconsin

# Etiquette and Protocol

### American Table Manners

http://www.cuisinenet.com/glossary/tableman.html

Detailed information on table manners for all occasions is available on this site. It includes the following articles: The Secrets of the Formal Place Setting, How to Use the Fork, Knife and Spoon, How to Use a Napkin, Tips and Pitfalls and What You Can Eat with Your Fingers. There is also a list of recommended books.

**Authority:** CyberPalate LLC

### Etiquette in Society

http://www.bartleby.com/95/

This is a full text version of Emily Post's 1922 edition. Use the search box or scroll down the page and access the material by chapter headings. Although the material is a bit dated, Emily Post's work is one of the underpinnings of modern American etiquette. This work is part of the larger Bartleby project website at http://www.bartleby.com.

**Authority:** Emily Post

### Net: User Guidelines and Netiquette

http://www.fau.edu/netiquette/net/netiquette.html

Detailed information on the whys and wherefores of interacting across the Net responsibly is the main thrust of this site. Definitely a must-read for all beginning users of the Internet, particularly the sections on Electronic Mail (e-mail), Electronic Communications, Discussion Groups and The Ten Commandments from the Computer Ethics Institute. Though the site was last updated in 1998, the information is as relevant now as it was four years ago. For instance, it is still good advice to "Never send or keep anything that you would mind seeing on the evening news."

**Authority:** Arlene Rinaldi, Florida Atlantic University

### Original Tipping Page

http://www.tipping.org/tips/TipsPageTipsUS.html

Part of the larger tipping.org site, this page has a long list of places you should tip including: the airport, barbershop, beauty shop, casino, cruise ship, deliveries, holidays, hotel, limousine, restaurant and more. Use the Quick Navigator or the Search boxes to access other parts of the site including tipping internationally and links to other sites.

**Authority:** The Original Tipping Page

### Robert's Rules of Order

http://www.constitution.org/rror/rror--00.htm

A great site for government classes, it has the full text of the 1915 version with modifications and enhancements from the 1996 edition. The first page is a table of contents with links to parts, articles and paragraphs.

**Authority:** General Henry M. Robert and the Constitution Society

# Flags (*see also* Atlases and International Country Information; Travel)

## Flag Etiquette

http://www.icss.com/usflag/flag.etiquette.html

This site gives information about how to display, handle, use and not use the Flag of the United States of America. Topics on this site include: Standards of Respect, Displaying the Flag Outdoors, Raising and Lowering the Flag, Displaying the Flag Indoors, Parading and Saluting the Flag, The Salute, The Pledge of Allegiance and National Anthem and The Flag in Mourning.

**Authority:** Duane Streufert

## Flags of all Countries

http://www.wave.net/upg/immigration/flags.html

Entries begin with a full color image of the flag and are arranged in alphabetic order by country. From the flag page you can access the following factual categories: Map, Geography, People, Government, Economy, Transportation, Communications and Defense. There are a few historical and non-country flags on this site.

**Authority:** Photius Coutsoukis and Information Technology Associates

## Flags of the Worlds

http://www.fotw.ca/flags/

Tied to a flag mailing list/discussion group, this site includes more than 9,900 pages and 18,500 images about flags. Many obscure or little known flags are included. FOTW is keyword-searchable or browsable using the table of contents.

**Authority:** Flags of the World

## World Flag Database

http://www.flags.net/

"There are over 260 pages on countries and international organizations. Each page contains basic information on the country, including its formal name, capital city, area, population, currency, languages and religions. The flags include the national and state flags, ensigns and sub-national flags. Where countries have changed their flags in the last few years the old flag is also shown." There are links to other flag sites, historical flags and a glossary.

**Authority:** The World Flag Database & Graham Bartram

# Full-Text Resources (*see also* History; Mythology; Reading and Literature)

## Alex Catalog of Electronic Texts

http://www.infomotions.com/alex/

The collection consists of American literature, English literature and Western philosophy. A simple search box is provided on the first page with a link to a more sophisticated search engine. Once a record or multiple records have been retrieved this site allows you to search within the full text of one or several items. There are three browsable lists: authors, titles and date.

**Authority:** Eric Lease Morgan, Infomotions, Inc.

## Archiving Early America

http://earlyamerica.com/

Click on Enter the World of Early America to access the full-text documents. The primary source documents on this site include newspapers, maps, magazines and other writings and are arranged under the following headings: The Declaration of Independence, The Constitution, The Bill of Rights, Milestone Events, Firsts! Pages from the Past, Maps, Writings, The Lives of Early Americans, Early American BookMarks, Notable Women of Early America and Gallery of Early American Portraits. An essay entitled "How To Read a 200 Year Old Document" is also included.

**Authority:** Archiving Early America

## Avalon Project

http://www.yale.edu/lawweb/avalon/avalon.htm

The Avalon Project has collected books, transcripts, charters and codes relating to Law, History and Diplomacy. Use the search feature to find documents within the entire collection. The documents are also browsable by time period: pre-18th Century, 18th Century, 19th Century and 20th Century. An alphabetic author/title list of all the documents is available on the site.

**Authority:** Law School, Yale University

## Bartleby.com

http://www.bartleby.com/

Bartleby.com Great Books Online, publishes full text fiction, nonfiction, verse and reference books on the Internet. It is keyword, author, title and subject searchable and browsable by type/category. Many useful reference books are available here including *The American Heritage Dictionary*, *Roget's II: The New Thesaurus* and *Bartlett's Familiar Quotations*.

**Authority:** Bartleby.com

## Children's Storybooks Online

http://www.magickeys.com/books/

This limited, full-text resource includes books for young children, older children and young adults. It is divided into six main sections: Books to Read, Sounds, Riddles, Maze and Coloring Book. Most of the full-text books are written by the owner of the site. (Grades K–8)

**Authority:** Carol Moore

## Classics for Young People

http://www.acs.ucalgary.ca/~dkbrown/storclas.html

A useful resource for both young people and teachers, this site indexes full-text Internet versions of classic novels. Currently there are more than 100 titles listed. This work is part of the larger Children's Literature Web Guide. (Grades 3–12) ∞

**Authority:** David K. Brown

## CMU Poetry Index

http://eserver.org/poetry/

This is a list of the full-text of many classic poems. The authors include Houseman, Dickinson, Angelou, Blake, Homer, Spenser and others.

**Authority:** Carnegie Mellon University

## Core Documents of the U.S. Democracy

http://www.access.gpo.gov/su_docs/locators/coredocs/

The Government Printing Office provides access to "the basic Federal Government documents that define our democratic society." The documents are divided into six areas: Legislative and Legal, Regulatory, Office of the President, Demographic, Economic and Miscellaneous. Within each section are documents such as the Gettysburg Address, Budget of the United States Government, Code of Federal Regulations and the Bill of Rights.

**Authority:** Government Printing Office

## Documenting the American South

http://docsouth.unc.edu/

The site states that it is "a full-text database of primary resources on Southern history, literature and culture from the colonial period through the first decades of the 20th century." It includes "three digitization projects: slave narratives, first-person narratives and Southern literature. A fourth, based on Confederate imprints, is in development." The collections are searchable or browsable by title or author list.

**Authority:** Academic Affairs Library, University of North Carolina, Chapel Hill

## DOUGLASS: Archives of American Public Address

http://douglass.speech.nwu.edu/

A unique full-text source that provides access to speech transcripts. Use the simple search box or browse through the following categories: Speaker, Title, Chronology or Issue. Movements include "Care for the Poor," "Human Rights," "Slavery" and "Temperance." The earliest speech in the archives is John Winthrop's "On Liberty" from 1645. The most recent speech is President William J. Clinton's, "Map Room Speech," August 17, 1998.

**Authority:** Douglass Project

## A Guide to the Book Arts and Book History on the World Wide Web

http://libraries.cua.edu/bookarts.html

"The page is designed to be a guide to Internet resources in the world of book arts and book history." The website links are arranged into the following categories: Academic Special Collections, Book Arts Courses & Exhibits, Booksellers, Discussion Lists & List Archives, Electronic Journals & Publications, Electronic Text & Imaging Projects, Finding Aids & WWW Guides, Government Organizations, Professional & Scholarly Organizations and Special Topics. ∞

**Authority:** Andrew K. Pace, Library and Information Science Library, The Catholic University of America

## Historical Text Archive

http://www.historicaltextarchive.com

This site "provides original material, links to other sites and electronic reprints of books and is organized by geography/nations and topics." Entries include articles, books, documents and photographs. ∞

**Authority:** Don Mabry, Professor of History, Associate Dean, Mississippi State University

## Internet Public Library: Online Texts Collection

http://www.ipl.org/reading/books/

Both fiction and nonfiction titles are included in this enormous full-text collection. There are over 17,000 full-text titles currently and more are added daily. Most of the texts are pre-1921 and in the public domain. The database is searchable by keyword or browsable by author, title or Dewey classification. The Dewey Decimal Classification® System allows browsing by subject areas such as Religion, Social Sciences, Technology, Geography and History. ∞

**Authority:** Internet Public Library

## Making of America

http://www.umdl.umich.edu/moa/

This "is a digital library of primary sources in American social history from the antebellum period through reconstruction." There are approximately 8,500 books and 50,000 journal articles with 19th century imprints in this collection. The pages of these items have been scanned in as images, so you are looking at a picture of each page, not a transcript. To access the images choose books or journals then search by keyword or browse by title or author.

**Authority:** University of Michigan and Cornell University

## National Archives: The Digital Classroom

http://www.nara.gov/education/classrm.html

"To encourage teachers of students at all levels to use archival documents in the classroom, the Digital Classroom provides materials from the National Archives and methods for teaching with primary sources." Click on Primary Sources and Activities to get to the heart of this site. The documents and teaching activities are arranged in chronological order beginning with Constitution Day and ending with an Inaugural Quiz.

**Authority:** National Archives and Records Administration

## The On-Line Books Page

http://digital.library.upenn.edu/books/

Over 14,000 full-text works are indexed on this site. The database can be searched or browsed by any of the following: New Listings, Author, Title, Library of Congress Subject or Serials. The easiest way to access the subjects in this database is by browsing by Library of Congress classification. Subjects such as Ethics, Etiquette, History, Geography, Music and Agriculture are included. This site complements and is similar to the Internet Public Library: Online Texts Collection annotated at left.

**Authority:** John Mark Ockerbloom

## Oxford Text Archive

http://ota.ahds.ac.uk/

The Oxford Text Archive contains over 2,500 books in 25 different languages. Search the catalog by choosing "The Catalog and Fulltext Search" from the first drop-down menu. There are other ways to search this site. Read the screens carefully to use the more advanced features like genre, period or format search.

**Authority:** Oxford Text Archive

## Perseus Project

http://www.perseus.tufts.edu/

The site states that it is a "digital library of resources for studying the ancient world. The library's materials include ancient texts and translations, philological tools, maps, extensively illustrated art catalogs and secondary essays on topics like vase painting." Use the simple search box or select a category such as Classics or English Renaissance from the table of contents.

**Authority:** Gregory Crane, Editor in Chief and Associate Professor of Classics, Tufts University

## Project Gutenberg

http://www.promo.net/pg/

Project Gutenberg was started in 1971 to promote the digitization of public domain full-text materials. It is probably one of the fastest growing full-text sites, boasting the addition of one e-text per day on average. Access the content by searching keyword, author or title or browse by author or title.

**Authority:** Project Gutenberg and Promo.net

# Genealogy (*see also* Biography)

## Ancestry

http://www.ancestry.com/

This site includes 2,500 databases containing genealogical information. Some of them require a paid subscription, but there are some free ones such as the Social Security Death Index (SSDI). The SSDI includes information such as Name, Born, Died, Residence, Last Benefit, SSN and State of Issue.

**Authority:** MyFamily.com Inc., The Social Security Administration for the SSDI.

## Cyndi's List

http://www.cyndislist.com/

This is a very popular starting point for genealogy research on the Internet. The directory consists of more than 100,000 annotated, regularly updated, cross-referenced links, which are arranged into 150 subject categories. The links go worldwide and are arranged both alphabetically and by topic. The site also contains a mailing list, a search engine and software to make personal genealogy home pages. ∞

**Authority:** Cyndi Howells

## FamilySearch

http://www.familysearch.com/

Sponsored by the LDS (Mormon) Church, FamilySearch provides free access to private family pedigrees, personal narratives, family organizations, public record information and the extensive genealogical records created by the Church and its members. There is a terrific guide to help you get started titled "How Do I Begin," a glossary and extensive help screens.

**Authority:** Church of Jesus Christ of Latter-Day Saints

### Genealogy Home Page

http://www.genhomepage.com/

Hundreds of links to genealogy sites have been organized on this page. Categories range from North American Genealogy Resources to Genealogy Software. This resource is affiliated with the Roots-L mailing list. ∞

**Authority:** Family Tree Maker Online

### Rand Genealogy Club

http://www.rand.org/personal/Genea/

A link site created and maintained by a group of Rand employees who share the genealogy hobby. The sizeable collection of genealogical resource links are divided into the following categories: RootsWeb Resources, Genealogy in the News, How to Start, Reference Information, Historical Information, Regional-Ethnic-Religious Groups, Computer and Internet, Miscellaneous, Recommended Generic Links and Surnames-Family-Trees-and-Databases. ∞

**Authority:** Rand Organization Employees

### Vital Records Information

http://vitalrec.com/index.html

This site contains information on how to obtain vital records and is arranged by state, territory and county of the United States. It includes addresses, costs and types of records available.

**Authority:** Webmaster@vitalrec.com

# Geology (*see also* Earth Science; Science; Science Fairs)

### Earthquake Hazards Program

http://earthquake.usgs.gov/

All kinds of earthquake information is accessible from this official United States Geologic Survey site. It is divided into the following categories: Latest Quake Info, General Quake Info, Hazards and Preparedness, Earthquake Research, Special Features, Additional Resources and Search. There are articles on topics such as famous earthquakes, locating earthquakes and listening to earthquakes. The latest quake information lists

locations and intensities of recent quakes along with some maps.

**Authority:** United States Geologic Survey

### Geologic Time Scale

http://www.ucmp.berkeley.edu/help/timeform.html

This page is the jumping-off point to a terrific compendium of geology information. The site begins with a graphic representation of the geologic time scale. Click on any era, period or eon to access information about that time. Every page off the time scale includes four buttons: stratigraphy, ancient life, tectonics and localities. "The Stratigraphy button will link to a page with information about stratigraphy, deposition, nomenclature and identification of member strata. Ancient Life will provide an overview of the major biological events, including origin and extinction of important groups. Tectonics will detail continental movements, changes in global ocean and atmospheric circulation and resulting changes in global climate." For information about specific fossils and fossil locations click on the "Localities" button.

**Authority:** Brian R. Speer, Robert Guralnick and Allen Collins, University of California, Berkeley

### Geysers

http://hoffman.wku.edu/geysers

This web page is a lengthy essay about Geysers. It includes links to other Geyser information resources. (Grades 5–Undergraduate)

**Authority:** Alan Glennon, Dept. of Geography and Geology, Western Kentucky University

### Landforms

http://www.athena.ivv.nasa.gov/curric/land/landform/landform.html

Articles and images are linked to the table of contents on this NASA-sponsored site. Included are topics such as mountains, alluvial fans, deltas, waterfalls, canyons, sand dunes and faults. ✎

**Authority:** SAIC, Kathee Terry and Martine Wayman

### Learning Web at the USGS

http://www.usgs.gov/education/

The Learning Web is provided by the U.S. Geological Survey and is "dedicated to K–12 education, exploration and lifelong learning." There are three main sections on this site. 1. Adventures in The Learning Web is a list of USGS educational materials. 2. Teaching in The Learning Web is a set of classroom activities and lessons. 3. Living in The Learning Web provides access to articles on topics that affect people every day and everywhere. (Grades K–12) ✎

**Authority:** United States Geological Survey

## Mineral and Gemstone Kingdom

http://www.minerals.net/

This site is a colorful compendium of minerals and gemstones. Extensive articles are found under the Minerals Resources section. These articles include information about identifying minerals, chemical properties and basic mineral geology. Other sections include Minerals A–Z, Gemstones, Gallery and Glossary. (Grades 7–Undergraduate)

**Authority:** Hershel Friedman

## The Mineral Gallery

http://mineral.galleries.com/default.htm

The gallery provides mineral images and descriptions. The site contents are listed by minerals, class or groupings. There is also a basic search feature. Entries average three paragraphs in length and include the chemical composition and physical characteristics of the mineral. A search function is also available. The pictures would be useful for anyone studying minerals. (Grades 7–Undergraduate)

**Authority:** Amethyst Galleries, Inc.

## Mineral Resources for Teachers

http://www.womeninmining.org/

This site by "Women In Mining is dedicated to educating students, teachers and the general public about the importance of minerals." The relevant information is arranged into many subject areas such as About Minerals, Activities, Games and Mineral Education Links. Within these areas are titles such as: Layer Cake Core Drilling, Rock Obituary, A Tour of Historical Rocks in Washington, DC, Minerals And You, Environmental Bingo Part I and Products. (Grades K–12) ✎

**Authority:** Women In Mining

## Mineralogy Database

http://webmineral.com/

Over 4,100 individual mineral species are described in this database. There are lists based on Dana's New classification and Strunz classification. Alphabetical listings of mineral species are available for browsing. Entries on specific minerals include a physical description, chemical composition and name origin. (High School–Undergraduate)

**Authority:** David Barthelmy

## Seismic Intensity Scales

http://www.museum.state.il.us/isas/kingdom/geo1001.html

Earthquakes are measured using either the Mercalli or the Richter intensity scale. These scales and their descriptions are arranged into two tables on this site.

**Authority:** Armando G. Amador

## Understanding Earthquakes

http://www.crustal.ucsb.edu/ics/understanding/

The contents of this site are arranged under the following headings: Quiz, Globe, Accounts, Rebound, History and Others. These categories include information on earthquake locations, articles about earthquakes, animation and illustrations.

**Authority:** Institute for Crustal Studies

## Virtual Cave

http://www.goodearthgraphics.com/virtcave.html

This site is comprised of essays and pictures of caves and cave features. It is organized into the following sections: Solution Caves, Lava Tube Caves, Sea Caves and Erosional Caves. Solution and Lava Tube Caves have the most extensive selection of pictures.

**Authority:** Dave Bunnell

## Volcano World

http://volcano.und.edu/

The place to go for information about volcanos. To access the site contents, browse by category such as World Region or Volcano Name or search by keyword. Articles include photos, maps, graphs and other information. Topics range from currently erupting volcanos to lava types. (Grades 7–Undergraduate) ✎

**Authority:** University of North Dakota

# Grammar, Writing and Style Guides (*see also* Dictionaries; Reference: Other Virtual Reference Sites; Thesauri)

## Blue Book of Grammar and Punctuation

http://www.grammarbook.com/

Based on the book by the same title, Jane Straus has created this site to assist writers with common grammar and punctuation problems. Choose from a category, and then scroll down the list of topics to find articles and examples.

**Authority:** Jane Straus

## Common Errors in English

http://www.wsu.edu/~brians/errors/

Ever wonder when to use "affect" or "effect?" This site answers this and many other questions about word usage. Also included are related links and information such as non-errors. According to the site non-errors are: "Those usages people keep telling you are wrong but which are actually standard in English."

**Authority:** Paul Brians, English Dept., Washington State University

## The Elements of Style

http://www.bartleby.com/141/

While this guide may be considered old (written in 1918) many of the rules are applicable today. The table of contents includes sections such as Elementary Rules of Usage, Elementary Rules of Composition, A Few Matters of Form, Words and Expressions Commonly Misused and Words Commonly Misspelled.

**Authority:** William Strunk

## Guide to Grammar and Writing

http://webster.commnet.edu/grammar/

This immense site on grammar, writing and usage is broken into the following sections: Word & Sentence Level; Paragraph Level; Essay & Research Paper Level; Ask Grammar, Quizzes, Search Devices; Peripherals & PowerPoints and GrammarPoll, Guestbook, Awards. These levels include definitions, descriptions, examples and some quizzes with answers.

**Authority:** Professor Charles Darling, Capital Community-Technical College

## On-Line English Grammar

http://www.edufind.com/english/grammar/toc.cfm

A table of contents page is the main entry point to this full-text grammar guide. Some of the sections in the guide are Nouns, Verbs, Determiners and Adjectives. Sound files for pronunciation of the alphabet are also available. The sound files use the British pronunciation. There is a subject index to the contents of the site and links to other Internet resources.

**Authority:** Anthony Hughes

## Study Guides and Strategies

http://www.iss.stthomas.edu/studyguides/

This guide to studying covers nine areas: Preparing to Learn, Studying, Classroom Participation, Reading Skills, Preparing for Tests, Taking Tests, Writing Basics, Math & Science and Webtruth. Under each area is a list of topics. Entries for the topic include an essay/or bulleted suggestion list and can include examples and links to other sources.

**Authority:** Joe Landsberger, Learning Center, University of St. Thomas

## Writing Guides on the Writing Center at Colorado State University

http://writing.colostate.edu/reference.htm

Probably the most extensive English grammar and writing guide, this site has mini-tutorials on many of different aspects of writing. The full-text of popular style guides such as APA, MLA and Chicago are available under the Working with Sources category. Other categories on the site include Writing Processes, Reading Processes, Types of Documents, Speeches & Presentations, Library, Internet and Field Research, Social Science and Qualitative Research and Working with Graphics and Tables.

**Authority:** Writing Center, Colorado State University

## Your Dictionary.Com: Grammars

http://www.yourdictionary.com/grammars.html

Grammars for languages as diverse as Cherokee and Coptic are available on this alphabetically arranged list. "You can look up the rules of a language and language courses where you can learn a new language. Additional language resources such as newspapers and on-line radio stations are linked to the appropriate language."

**Authority:** yourDictionary.com Inc.

# Grants, Grant Making and Nonprofit Organizations

## Foundations and Grant Makers

http://www.foundations.org/grantmakers.html

This is a simple list of sites relating to foundations and grant makers. Types of organizations included in this directory are Charities, Attorneys Specializing in Nonprofits, Government Grants and Related Sites. ∞

**Authority:** Northern California Community Foundation Inc.

## Foundation Center Online

http://www.fdncenter.org/

The Foundation Center provides this comprehensive grant site. It includes information for both the grant seeker and the giver. In the Learning Lab are extensive articles on how to write a grant and acquire funding. The site is keyword-searchable.

**Authority:** The Foundation Center

## Guidestar

http://www.guidestar.org/

A searchable database of more than 700,000 U.S. non-profit organizations is the centerpiece of this site. There are articles such as "How to Be a Better More Effective Nonprofit Manager" or "Organization and Information on Finances." There is also information on the activities of both donor organizations and nonprofit organizations.

**Authority:** Philanthropic Research Inc.

# Health and Medicine (*see also* Nutrition)

### AMA Physician Select

http://www.ama-assn.org/aps/amahg.htm

"Physician Select is intended for use by the general public to allow them quick access to information on physicians." It is "compiled and published by the American Medical Association (AMA) as a reference source of demographic and professional information on individual physicians in the United States." After reading and accepting the disclaimer, you can search for physician information by name or medical specialty.

**Authority:** American Medical Association

### Complete Home Medical Guide

http://cpmcnet.columbia.edu/texts/guide/

This is an electronic copy of the third revised print edition. From the text menu the book is divided into six sections: Using Your Health Care System, New Approaches to Wellness, Symptoms & Diagnoses, First Aid & Safety, Treatment & Prevention of Disease and Drugs & Their Use.

**Authority:** Columbia University College of Physicians and Surgeons

### Hardin Meta Directory of Internet Health Resources

http://www.lib.uiowa.edu/hardin/md/

According to the site "Hardin MD is a 'list of lists.' Its purpose is to provide easy access to comprehensive resource lists in health-related subjects. It includes subject listings in large 'one-stop-shopping' sites, such as MedWeb and Yahoo and also independent discipline-specific lists. Hardin MD subject pages indicate the length of lists in each subject, making it easy to see at a glance which lists are most comprehensive. These are often not the lists from the 'one-stop-shopping' sites, but those developed by people within the field, which are well-known and frequently cited within the field, but not well-known outside it." Use the search box or browse through the subject lists.

**Authority:** Hardin Library for the Health Sciences, University of Iowa

### HealthWeb

http://healthweb.org/

The goal for this site is to "collect and provide links to evaluated, quality information on the Internet and to meet the health information needs of consumers and health professionals." An alphabetic list of subjects provides access to the entries in the database. Each topical entry has a page with information, such as related organizations, publications and resources. ∞

**Authority:** HealthWeb

### Heart: An Online Exploration

http://www.fi.edu/biosci/heart.html

This is a descriptive and pictorial tour of the human heart. It includes separate pages for heart development, structure and blood vessels. There is information available on how to have a healthy heart, how to monitor your heart's health and a look at the history of heart science.

**Authority:** The Franklin Institute Science Museum

### KidsHealth

http://kidshealth.org/

Hundreds of articles, resources and features are organized under the following categories: For Parents, For Teens and For Kids. Topics for the extensive articles include, first aid, positive parenting, emotions and behavior, dealing with feelings and kids' health problems among others. (Grades 3–12)

**Authority:** The Nemours Foundation

### Medical Matrix

http://www.medmatrix.org/index.asp

This database requires a free registration to use and tends to be a bit scholarly, but the resources are invaluable if you are looking for accurate information. Information is organized into the following categories: Specialties, Diseases, Clinical Practice, Literature, Education, Healthcare & Professionals, Medical Computing, Internet & Technology and Marketplace. Each category is further subdivided into sections like textbooks, directories, educational materials and full-text. Thousands of Internet sites are contained in the keyword-searchable database.

**Authority:** Medical Matrix

### Neuroscience for Kids

http://faculty.washington.edu/chudler/neurok.html

"This home page has been created for all students and teachers who would like to learn more about the nervous system. Enjoy the activities and experiments on your way to learning more about the brain and spinal cord." Activities include making a model of the brain, a neuron or the retina, coloring pictures, solving puzzles and playing games. (Grades 5–High School)

**Authority:** Eric H. Chudler, Ph.D.

### The NLM Gateway

http://gateway.nlm.nih.gov/gw/Cmd

The Gateway searches MEDLINE/PubMed, OLDMEDLINE, LOCATORplus, MEDLINEplus, DIRLINE, AIDS Meetings, Health Services Research Meetings, Space Life Sciences Meetings and HSRProj. Reading the "Overview" is recommended. These databases are citation or bibliographic indexes and do not contain the actual journal articles.

**Authority:** National Library of Medicine

### PubMed

http://www.ncbi.nlm.nih.gov/PubMed

This is the National Library of Medicine's page for access to MEDLINE and Pre-Medline, the premier medical journal article database. Actual journal articles are not available from this site. Article citations date back to 1966.

**Authority:** National Library of Medicine

### RxList

http://www.rxlist.com

Drug products currently on the U.S. market or close to approval are all listed here. Entries contain the following information: Description, Action, Use, Warnings, Precautions, Drug Interactions, Side Effects, Toxicity and Dosing. To find a specific drug, search by keyword.

**Authority:** RxList.com

# History (*see also* Biography; Full-Text Resources)

### Abzu: Guide to Resources for the Study of the Ancient Near East

http://www-oi.uchicago.edu/OI/DEPT/RA/ABZU/ABZU.HTML

The Oriental Institute has attempted to gather links to all of the websites relating to the Ancient Near East onto one organized site. There are two types of indexes on this site. The first are Primary Indexes which are arranged by author, project or institutional affiliation. The second are Secondary Indexes which are arranged by topic such as directories, museum collections online, Egypt and Mesopotamia. While there is some overlap between the two types of indexes, the Primary Indexes are not completely contained in the Secondary Indexes. ∞

**Authority:** Oriental Institute, University of Chicago

### Celebration of Black History

http://www.rockingham.k12.va.us/EMS/BlackHistory/BlackHistory.html

This page was created as a celebration of Black History Month and contains a wealth of information relating to African-American history. It is a list of annotated links arranged by date. The date ranges include: 1619–1863, 1929–1954, 1863–1896, 1954–1997, 1896–1929 and All Time Periods.

**Authority:** Linda Ervin

### CircusWeb! Circuses Present and Past

http://www.circusweb.com/circuswebFrames.html

The CircusWeb is divided into the following sections: About, Circuses, History, Lore and Fans. The use of frames makes content appear to be part of CircusWeb, when in fact it is not. For Example, click on Circuses to bring up a linked list of circuses. Each of the circuses listed here have their own home pages but appear embedded in the frame. Use Netscape's right click "Open Frame in New Window" function to break out of the frame. The information in the History, Lore and Fans sections is content created by CircusWeb and includes brief articles on topics such as The Circus Tent, Circus Terms and Circus Superstitions.

**Authority:** Graphics 2000 and Intelligent Software Associates, Inc.

### Comparative Chronology of Money from Ancient Times to the Present Day

http://www.ex.ac.uk/~RDavies/arian/amser/chrono.html

This site is closely tied to one of the site author's books. It does provide a wonderful outline to the history of money. Go to the bottom of the page to access the clickable timeline which begins with 9,000 BC and ends with AD 2002. Events significant to the development, use and history of money are related in one or two sentences on the timeline charts. (Grades 7–12)

**Authority:** Roy Davies and Glyn Davies

## dMarie Time Capsule

http://www.dmarie.com/timecap/

Type in a year, month and day and retrieve everything from headlines to consumer prices. The site currently has data online for the years 1800 to the present, "although data for the years 1800–1875 is probably spotty."

**Authority:** dMarie Direct Inc.

## Footnotes to History

http://users.mcleodusa.net/j/jlerwin/index.htm

Subtitled "The nations you didn't learn about in high school geography," this site provides "an overview of ephemeral states, micronations, secessionist states and every other kind of country you never heard of in high school." It is organized by Subject, Sources and Links and includes everything from Maryland in Africa to the Republic of West Florida.

**Authority:** James L. Erwin

## General History Sources

http://www.execpc.com/~dboals/hist-gen.html

Created for K–12 teachers, this index sorts hundreds of sites on the Web into the following areas: General Guides, Topical History, Chronological Areas, People and the Individual in History (Oral History), Regional Sources/Studies, Museums, Archives, Professional Organizations and Discussion Lists, Skills: Teaching and Learning History, Software Sources and Journals. (Grades K–12) ∞

**Authority:** Dennis Boals

## H-Net Humanities & Social Sciences OnLine

http://h-net2.msu.edu/

This site has the "objective of advancing teaching and research in the arts, humanities and social sciences." Click on the category Teaching to access the collection of "teaching resources including teaching focused discussion networks, H-Net regional teaching centers, syllabi, links, conference papers on multimedia teaching and web-based teaching projects." (High School–Undergraduate)

**Authority:** H-Net

## Histor eSearch.com

http://www.snowcrest.net/jmike/

"This site is intended for use by students, educators and history buffs. All resources and links to this site have been previewed for quality of academic content." Hundreds of web pages are indexed on this site and have been divided into subject categories such as U.S.

History, Ancient World History, Asian History, News and Sports and Rock & Roll.

**Authority:** Michael Jenkins, Histor eSearch.com

## Historic Audio Archives

http://webcorp.com/civilrights/

The archive is organized into five sections. Section one: Rogues 'n' Heroes at the RealAudio Gallery includes "RealAudio from some of the most interesting people of our time." Section two: The Richard Nixon Audio Archive includes "Samples from Nixon's greatest hits." Section three: Neville Chamberlain and Adolf Hitler, Fall, 1938, also includes "WWII clips from Churchill and FDR." Section four: Voices of the Civil Rights Era includes tapes from "JFK, MLK and Malcolm X." And finally section five: More Historic Sound Clips includes Clinton, Bush, Liddy, Quayle and more." (High School–Undergraduate)

**Authority:** Webcorp

## History—American and British

http://www.libraries.rutgers.edu/rul/rr_gateway/research_guides/history/history.shtml

Sponsored by Rutgers University Library, the goal of this page is to "provide a searchable structure for the scholarly resources of American and British history available on the Internet." It is arranged into the following sections: Reference Resources, Archival and MSS. Guides, General History Portals, Sites Organized by Subject, Sites Organized by Period, Full-text Documents by Period and History Associations & History Listservs. ∞

**Authority:** Stanley D. Nash PhD and Tom Glynn, Rutgers University

## History of Handwriting and the Story of the Fountain Pen

http://www.parkerpen.co.uk/history/

"The story of western writing spans over 25,000 years of history and provides the backdrop to many other interesting topics." This site delivers information about topics such as cave painting, hieroglyphs, calligraphy, tools, pens and pencils and is heavily illustrated.

**Authority:** Parker Pens

## History Sources for Europe/Russia/Eastern Europe

http://www.geocities.com/dboals.geo/europe.html

Created for K–12 teachers, this site indexes hundreds of sites relating to European history. They are arranged into the following categories: Ancient and Classical, Perseus Sites, Medieval, Renaissance/Reformation,

Modern/Contemporary, Russia, Regional/National, Special (Western Imperialism, World War I, World War II, Holocaust) and General/Miscellaneous. (Grades K–12) ∞

**Authority:** Dennis Boals

### Horus' History Links

http://www.ucr.edu/h-gig/horuslinks.html

The purpose of this site is to "introduce the diversity of educational and research resources available on the Web not ordinarily consulted by historians and history students. Such sites include antique and decorator catalogues, real estate ads for historical properties, postcards, genealogy resources, local historical societies, museums outside the U.S., travel agency and tourism information and nonprofessional and avocational historical organizations." The site consists of the following six sections: Histories of Specific Countries, Times and Places; Areas of History; On-line Services About History; Web Tools; Alphabetical Listing of Link Collections and Search the HORUS Database. All websites in the index can be browsed alphabetically or by category. Additionally a keyword-searchable database is available. ∞

**Authority:** Dept. of History, University of California, Riverside

### Maritime History on the Internet

http://ils.unc.edu/maritime/

The goal of this site is not necessarily to provide comprehensive coverage of Maritime websites on the net, but to provide access to "valuable and interesting sources." The resources are divided into categories such as Researching a Ship, Modern Sailing and Nautical Archaeology. ∞

**Authority:** Peter McCracken, Library, Univ. of Washington

### Non-Western History

http://www.execpc.com/~dboals/hist.html

This site indexes web pages relating to history for non-western cultures. It is arranged by geographic regions including: Asia/Pacific, Central/South America, China/Japan, Africa, Middle East, India and General/Cross-Cultural. There are more than 600 sites indexed on this page. (Grades K–12) ∞

**Authority:** Dennis Boals

### Timelines of History

http://timelines.ws/

The Timeline does not index the Web, rather it tries to list all-important events and their dates in order. Click on one of the year ranges such as 1 AD to 299 AD or

1898–1899 to access brief data about famous people, famous events and other historical events.

**Authority:** Algis Ratnikas

### World History

http://www.hyperhistory.com/

This site is a synchronoptical chart, which means "Seeing at the same time." This chart "provides a perspective of world historical events and enables the reader to hold simultaneously in mind of what was happening in widely separated parts of the earth." Click on HyperHistory Online to access the chart's main page, then select People, History, Events or Maps. There are more than 2,000 files and several hundred links on this site.

**Authority:** Andreas Nothiger

### WWW Virtual Library: History Central Catalogue

http://history.cc.ukans.edu/history/VL/

One of the most comprehensive directories to history resources on the Internet, the Central Catalogue is organized into four main sections. These sections are Research: Methods and Materials, By Countries and Regions, Eras and Epochs and Historical Topics. Thousands of sites are indexed including topics such as Tibet, Slavery and Software.

**Authority:** Lynn H. Nelson, University of Kansas

## History: Ancient and Medieval

### Ancient World Web

http://www.julen.net/ancient/

One of the oldest history sites on the Web, Ancient World Web has been around since 1994. It is updated and maintained regularly and contains more than 1,100 links. Categories include such diverse topics as Daily Life, Institutions and Organizations and Science. ∞

**Authority:** Julia Hayden

### Exploring Ancient World Cultures

http://eawc.evansville.edu/eawcindex.htm

This site is a complex and comprehensive index of websites relating to ancient and medieval times. "It is divided into five sub-indices: a chronology, an essay index, an image index, an Internet site index and a primary text index. Each of these is further divided into sections, one for each of the cultures represented: the Near East, India, Egypt, China, Greece, Rome, Early Islam and Medieval Europe." The site is also keyword-searchable. ∞

**Authority:** Exploring Ancient World Cultures.

## Internet Medieval Sourcebook

http://www.fordham.edu/halsall/sbook.html

The Sourcebook organizes links to thousands of websites into three major sections on this site. These sections are Selected Sources, Full Text Sources and Saint's Lives. This page is a part of the ORB (Online Reference Book for Medieval Studies) site at http://orb.rhodes.edu. There are two other related sourcebooks: Ancient History Sourcebook at http://www.fordham.edu/halsall/ancient/asbook.html and Modern History Sourcebook at http://www.fordham.edu/halsall/mod/modsbook.html. ∞

**Authority:** Paul Halsall, editor ORB

## Search Argos

http://argos.evansville.edu/

The goal here is to "create an academically viable resource for students, teachers and scholars of the ancient and medieval worlds." To do this, they have created relationships with other websites (associate sites) that organize, evaluate and find content-related to ancient and medieval history. Argos then indexes the contents of these associate sites and makes them available via the search engine. ∞

**Authority:** Anthony F. Beavers and Hiten Sonpal

## WWW Medieval Resources

http://ebbs.english.vt.edu/medieval/

A guide to Medieval websites, this site is organized by topics, including Discussion Lists & Information, Links to Texts from and about the Medieval Period, Medieval History, Archeology, & Architecture, Links to Databases, Links to other Home Pages, Links to Archives of MSS Facsimiles, Art, etc., Medieval Sciences, Libraries and Links to Miscellaneous Materials. From these topics, a wealth of materials including graphics, full-text, primary, secondary and other curricular sources can be found. ∞

**Authority:** Dan Mosser, Virginia Polytechnic Institute and State University

# History: United States (see also Biography; Full Text Resources)

## American Cultural History—The Twentieth Century

http://www.nhmccd.edu/contracts/lrc/kc/decades.html

"The purpose of these pages is to present a series of web guides on the decades of the twentieth century," according to the site. This page is arranged into ten-year sections from 1900 to 1999. Each section includes brief facts, statistics and informational paragraphs with links to outside sources and bibliographies.

**Authority:** Peggy Whitley, Kingwood College Library

## American History 102: 1865–Present

http://us.history.wisc.edu/hist102/

This site has been designed as a companion to a college course of the same name. The site has organized a guide to American History on the World Wide Web by topic under the Hitchhiker's Guide to American History section. The Who's Who in American History section includes biographies for historical figures arranged into four areas: names, eras, occupations and photos. (Undergraduate)

**Authority:** Stanley K. Schultz, Professor of History, William P. Tishler and Shane Hamilton

## American Memory from the Library of Congress

http://lcweb2.loc.gov/ammem/ammemhome.html

Over seven million items including text documents, videos and photographs are organized into more than 100 rich historical collections. Some of the collection titles are: Baseball Cards, California Folk Music and The Federal Writers Project. To access these collections, browse by subject under the Collection Finder heading. To search for specific items, click on the Search heading. The Learning Page heading accesses lesson ideas, activities, tools and other information about using the collections.

**Authority:** Library of Congress

## American Studies Web

http://www.georgetown.edu/crossroads/asw/

The American Studies Web includes hundreds of websites. Click on the search link to access a list of topics that range from the Diaspora to Visual Culture. Each site listed includes a brief annotation.

**Authority:** David Phillips, Michael Coventry, Jamie Poster and Edward Maloney, Georgetown University

## America's West, Development & History

http://www.AmericanWest.com/

This comprehensive site on the American West includes articles which are several paragraphs in length, illustrations, maps and links to other websites. Scroll down the home page to find: American Westward Expansion, Native American Tribes and Nations, European Emigration, Gunslingers and Outlaws, Pioneer Towns, Forts and Other Places, Western Pioneers, Frontiermen,

Mountain Men and Fur Traders, Women of the West, American Archaeology, Cowboys and Music.

**Authority:** American West

## Colonial America 1600–1775 K–12 Resources

http://falcon.jmu.edu/~ramseyil/colonial.htm

This site indexes other Internet sites about the Colonial Period. It has been created for the K–12 audience and is organized into the categories such as history, maps, lesson plans, cooking, holidays and Indians of North America. (Grades K–12)

**Authority:** Inez Ramsey, Professor Emeritus Library Science Program, James Madison University

## Crossroads, A K–16 American History Curriculum

http://ericir.syr.edu/Virtual/Lessons/crossroads/

Crossroads is a history lesson plan page which is divided into the following categories: Background Material, Essays, Elementary Curriculum, Middle School Curriculum, High School Curriculum and Postsecondary Curriculum. The curricula are arranged to include topics that begin with discovery of America and end with the present day. Lesson plans, activities, essays and links are provided. (Grades K–Undergraduate)

**Authority:** Henry E. Mueller and Stephen L. Schechter, Project Directors

## History Sources for North America/Canada

http://www.geocities.com/dboals.geo/amer.html

This site has been created for K–12 teachers. It indexes hundreds of U.S. and Canadian history sites on the Web into the areas such as The Civil War, Imperialism and Oral History/Folklore. This is part of the History/Social Studies for K–12 Teachers site found at http://www.execpc.com/~dboals/boals.html (Grades K–12)

**Authority:** Dennis Boals

## Hypertext on American History from Revolution to Reconstruction

http://www.let.rug.nl/usanew

This page was originally created as a means of teaching students to write HTML and use computers. Since it was being taught to American Studies students, American history was used as the subject for the pages. It is a wonderful resource for U.S. history especially since it is written from an international perspective. It includes many full-text documents and essays. An outline format is used to access the full-text articles. Topics for the articles range from "Foreign Rule Breaks Down in the Colonial Period" to "The McCarthy Era in Modern America." This site also includes biographies for notable Americans and presidential information such as speeches and writings.

**Authority:** George M. Welling, Project Coordinator, Dept. of Alfa-Informatica, University of Groningen

## Oregon Trail

http://www.isu.edu/~trinmich/Oregontrail.html

Created as a companion to the documentary video "The Story of the Oregon Trail," this site contains many resources for teaching and learning about the trail. It includes a lengthy primer titled "All About the Oregon Trail," a list of "Historic Sites on the Trail" complete with photos and descriptions, a collection of short anecdotes and charts under the heading "Fantastic Facts About the Oregon Trail," a "Trail Archive" containing full text of trail diaries and books, videos, audiotapes and computer games under the heading "Shop the Oregon Trail."

**Authority:** Mike Trinklein and Steve Boettcher

## United States Civil War Center

http://www.cwc.lsu.edu/

The mission of this site is "to locate, index and make available all appropriate private and public data regarding the Civil War," and to "promote the study of the Civil War from all the perspectives of all professions, occupations and academic disciplines." Use the search engine or the browse index to locate pages on topics such as archaeology, flags, diaries and historic places.

**Authority:** David Madden, Director, United States Civil War Center, Louisiana State University

## United States History Out Loud

http://www.hpol.org/

The site currently includes audio materials on the following people: Rev. Martin Luther King, President Franklin Delano Roosevelt, Sir Winston Churchill, Secretary of State George Marshall, President Lyndon Baines Johnson, President John F. Kennedy, President Bill Clinton and more. Transcripts of the speeches are included. Audio materials are from presidential libraries and other archives.

**Authority:** History Out Loud, The Challenge of Democracy

# History: World Wars I & II (see also Biography; Full Text Resources)

### Teacher's Guide to the Holocaust

http://fcit.coedu.usf.edu/Holocaust/

"An overview of the people and events of the Holocaust through photographs, documents, art, music, movies and literature." This site is arranged into five main sections: Timeline, People, The Arts, Student Activities and Teacher Resources. Lengthy articles with illustrations and web links are the centerpiece. Titles include Perpetrators, Survivors, the Rise of the Nazi Party, Resistance, Music and Literature. The Student Activities section contains a list of lesson plans and web links for studying the Holocaust. The Teacher Resources section contains bibliographies for articles, books, documents, films, images and software related to the Holocaust. A glossary is also available from the Teacher Resources section. (Grades K–12)

**Authority:** Florida Center for Instructional Technology, College of Education, University of South Florida

### World War I Document Archive

http://www.lib.byu.edu/~rdh/wwi/

This World War I archive "is international in focus and intends to present in one location primary documents concerning the Great War." There are nine divisions to this page including: Conventions, Treaties & Official Papers; Documents by Year; Memorials, Personal Reminiscences; WWI Biographical Dictionary; WWI Image Archive; Special Topics and Commentaries; The Maritime War; The Medical Front and WWI Sites: Links to Other Resources.

**Authority:** Jane Plotke PhD, The World War I Document Archive

### World War I: Trenches on the Web

http://www.worldwar1.com/

Page down this site to find the Good Starting Points and Other Items of Interest sections. These two points include links to articles, trivia, sound files, artwork, biographies, maps, country information, timelines and other World War I-related information.

**Authority:** Mike Iavarone

### World War II on the Web

http://web.uccs.edu/~history/index/worldwar2.html

Subtitled a "Guide to Resources & Research on the Web," this website indexes hundreds of links. It includes sections ranging from general resources to the European and Pacific theaters.

**Authority:** Dept. of History, University of Colorado at Colorado Springs

# Hoaxes, Myths and Urban Legends

### AFU & Urban Legends Archive

http://www.urbanlegends.com/

AFU stands for alt.folklore.urban which is a USENET group that discusses Urban Legends. Scroll down the page for a grid of Urban Legend Topics such as Food, Death, Disney, Products, Songs and Movies. The site is searchable, and there are links to related web pages.

**Authority:** AFU and Jason R. Heimbaugh

### HOAX Warnings

http://www.Europe.Datafellows.com/news/hoax.htm

HOAX Warnings is an easy-to-use site with information about virus hoaxes. You can find specific hoaxes by browsing the alphabetical or latest lists. Alternately, you can search the descriptions database by keyword.

**Authority:** Datafellows

### HoaxBusters

http://hoaxbusters.ciac.org/

"A public service of the CIAC Team and the U.S. Department of Energy," this site includes information on hoaxes, chain letters, the history of hoaxes and how to recognize hoaxes. There are buttons at the top of the page including: Hoax Info, Hoax Categories, Hoax Index and Hoax Search. My favorite hoaxes can be found using the Hoax Categories button. The category is titled "Jokes" with the subtext: "Warning messages that it's hard to believe that anyone would believe." Scroll down the first page of this site to access a list of other hoax pages.

**Authority:** CIAC Team

### Symantec Security Updates

http://www.symantec.com/avcenter/

Symantec is the producer of Norton Anti-Virus software. This web page lists new viruses and the solutions Symantec has created. Scroll down the page to find the Virus Encyclopedia, Hoaxes and Jokes sections. The Virus Encyclopedia has brief articles including how to remove them for all known viruses. The Hoaxes and Jokes sections are simple lists by name of supposed virus including Doh, Wobbling and Zlatko.

**Authority:** Symantec

### Urban Legends Reference Pages

http://www.snopes2.com/

Hundreds of urban legends are arranged into broad categories such as Horror, Titanic, Toxin du Jour, Automobiles and Christmas. The essays are several paragraphs in length and provide links to other resources where appropriate. The site is searchable and there is a site map for browsing.

**Authority:** Barbara and David P. Mikkelson

### Vmyths

http://www.vmyths.com

Originally titled "Computer Virus Myths" the foundations of this site began in 1988 with the publication of an article and then a website. Along with comprehensive descriptions and links of Hoaxes, Myths and Urban Legends are articles on topics such as "How to Spot a Virus Hoax" and "False Authority Syndrome." The site is keyword-searchable or browsable via the Hoaxes A–Z index.

**Authority:** Vmyths and Rhode Island Soft Systems, Inc.

# International Country Information (see also Atlases and Maps; Flags; Travel; Statistics)

### Chiefs of State and Cabinet Members of Foreign Governments

http://www.odci.gov/cia/publications/chiefs/

This CIA-sponsored site is arranged in alphabetical order. Each country listing links to a single page. The pages contain a list of the chiefs of state and cabinet members for each country.

**Authority:** U.S. Central Intelligence Agency

### CIA World Factbook

http://www.odci.gov/cia/publications/factbook/

This factbook is prepared by the Central Intelligence Agency (CIA) for use by U.S. officials. It contains an alphabetic list of countries, islands, oceans and regions. Each entry from the list includes a map, statistics and information in the following categories: Geography, People, Government, Economy, Communications, Transportation, Military and Transnational Issues.

**Authority:** U.S. Central Intelligence Agency

### The Library of Congress Country Studies

http://lcweb2.loc.gov/frd/cs/cshome.html

Scroll down the page to find an alphabetic listing of Country Studies books that are available online. These books start with a clickable table of contents which is several pages long. There is extensive information about the history, the society and environment, the politics and government, the economy and the country's geography. Not all of the countries in the world are currently on this list, but it is growing.

**Authority:** U.S. Federal Research Division, Library of Congress, Country Studies/Area Handbook Program, Dept. of the Army

### E-Conflict World Encyclopedia

http://www.emulateme.com/

The goal of this site is to "Eradicate Conflict by increasing cultural awareness." Countries are arranged in alphabetical order. Information on each country includes: Economy, Defense, Geography, Government, History, People and National Anthem.

**Authority:** Emulate Me

### Encyclopedia of the Orient

http://i-cias.com/e.o/index.htm

The geographic focus of this site "covers all countries and cultures between Mauritania in the west and Iran in the east, Turkey in the north and Sudan in south." Content is written specifically for this site and includes more than 600 articles. Choose a country or topic from the list on the right, or use the keyword search box.

**Authority:** LexicOrient

### ICL Country Index

http://www.uni-wuerzburg.de/law/home.html

The International Constitutional Law site provides the full-text of constitutions from countries around the world. It is organized alphabetically by country. Each entry provides information relating to: history and news, constitutional background and political parties. Links to other country information are provided for some nations.

**Authority:** A. Tschentscher, University at Wurzburg, Denmark

### United Nations

http://www.un.org/

This is the Official United Nations website. This is an amazing full-text resource of information about U.N. activities and resources. It is available in several languages including English, French, Spanish, Russian, Chinese and Arabic. Some of the major categories on the site are Peace & Security, Economic & Social Development, Human Rights, Humanitarian Affairs and International Law.

**Authority:** United Nations Dept. of Public Information

### U.S. Department of State

http://www.state.gov/r/pa/bgn/

Organized into a simple list, Background Notes provide information on geographic entities and international organizations. Background Notes for some countries are unavailable. The Notes include sections on: People, History, Government, Political Conditions, Economy, Defense, Foreign Relations, U.S. Relations and Travel/Business. Older editions are archived on the site.

**Authority:** U.S. Dept. of State

## Legal Information

### AllLaw

http://www.alllaw.com/

An easy-to-use site, AllLaw provides access to the U.S. Code and many other directories organizations and law review resources under headings such as Legal Organizations, Federal Resources, Schools & Education, Legal Practice Information, Journals & Periodicals, Community & Culture, Business and more. There are State Court Cases available but the comprehensiveness varies greatly between the states.

**Authority:** AllLaw.com

### Findlaw

http://www.findlaw.com

This site is a directory and database of legal materials on the Internet. Primary legal materials such as codes, case law and regulations can be found under Cases & Codes, U.S. Federal Resources and U.S. State Resources sections of the site. Secondary legal materials such as law journals, treatises and commentary can be found under News & Reference and Legal Practice Materials sections of the site. Other items in the index include directories, legal mailing lists, law firms, law schools and international legal resources. ∞

**Authority:** FindLaw

### Lawyers.com

http://www.lawyers.com/

More than 420,000 attorneys and firms are listed in this directory. Search by practice specialty, city and/or state. Also has sections called About the Law and Law Today. The site allows the user to find a lawyer, learn about the law and know their legal options.

**Authority:** Martindale-Hubbell

### Legal Information Institute—Supreme Court Collection

http://supct.law.cornell.edu:8080/supct

Most, if not all, of the Federal Supreme Court decisions since May of 1990 and all pending cases since the October 1998 term are included in this database. In addition, 610 key historic cases are also available. There are many different access points to the collection. It is searchable by keyword or browsable by date of decision. Historic information is arranged by topic, party name and opinion author.

**Authority:** U.S. Supreme Court and Legal Information Institute

### Nolo's Legal Encyclopedia

http://www.nolo.com/encyclopedia/

Search the encyclopedia by keyword or browse the following categories: Small Business, Employment, Patent, Copyright & Trademark, Courts & Mediation, Legal Research, Parents & Children, Spouses & Partners, Older Americans, Legal Dictionary, Wills & Estate Planning, Consumer, Debt & Credit, Tax Problems, Real Estate, Landlords & Tenants, Personal Injury and General Issues. Articles under these categories are excerpted from Nolo books and while the goal may be to sell their own books the articles are valid and valuable in their own right.

**Authority:** Nolo Publishing

### Oyez Project—U.S. Supreme Court Multimedia Database

http://oyez.nwu.edu

This project "provides abstracts and other materials for leading cases in constitutional law decided by the Supreme Court of the United States." You can search for cases by Title, Citation, Subject or Date. There are hundreds of hours worth of oral argument sound recordings on this site along with "dozens of panoramic images of the Supreme Court Building." Current and past Justices are listed along with biographical information.

**Authority:** Jerry Goldman, Northwestern University

## Librarianship: Professional Resources

### ACQWeb

http://acqweb.library.vanderbilt.edu/

Acquisitions Web has been on the Internet since 1994 and is said to be the most useful site on the Web for librarians. ACQWeb provides comprehensive access to resources such as publisher lists, book review sites, library school lists, preservation and binding web pages and general reference resources. The site is divided into 11 major sections: Web News for Inquiring Minds, Verification Tools and Resources, AcqWeb's Directory of Publishers and Vendors, Associations and Organizations, Library and Information Science, Journals, Newsletters and Electronic Discussion Archives, Reference Resources, Guides to Getting Started on the Web, ACQNET, the Edited Listserv, AcqWeb Information and Credits.

**Authority:** Anna Belle Leiserson, Collection Development Librarian, Vanderbilt Law Library

## Cataloger's Reference Shelf

http://www.tlcdelivers.com/tlc/crs/CRS0000.htm

This useful site delivers the full text to 21 manuals originally produced by the Library of Congress along with several other reference works. The manuals include: Bibliographic Data, Holdings Data, Descriptive Cataloging of Rare Books and LCSH: Principles of Structure and Policies for Application.

**Authority:** Library Corporation

## Librarian's Yellow Pages

http://www.LibrariansYellowPages.com/

More than 1,000 listings are available in this easy-to-use directory. It is keyword-searchable or browsable using any of the following lists: Audio & Video, Automation, Books & Periodicals, CD-ROMs & Software, Equipment, Furnishings & Supplies, Internet/Online, Services, Children's Y.A. & School Librarian's Resource Guide, Law Librarian's Resource Guide and Impossible to Find—Library Resource Information.

**Authority:** Raissa Fomerand, MLS and The Librarian's Yellow Pages

## Publishers' Catalogs

http://www.lights.com/publisher

This practical site tries to list every publisher's catalog that is available via the Internet. The site is keyword-searchable and browsable geographically by City, State, Country, US—Alphabetic or All (7,000+). You can also browse by topic such as science or by type of material such as magazines.

**Authority:** Northern Lights Internet Solutions Ltd.

# Libraries

## LibDex—The Library Index

http://www.libdex.com/

This site indexes more than 17,000 libraries. "Libdex is a worldwide directory of library homepages, web-based OPACs, Friends of the Library pages and library e-commerce affiliate links," says the site introduction. It also includes listings for OPAC vendors, publishers and articles on fundraising. The directory does not include links to terminal-based OPACs.

**Authority:** Peter Scott, Northern Lights Internet Solutions Ltd.

## Library of Congress

http://www.loc.gov

If you think the Library of Congress is just another book catalog, think again. The main page has information on and/or links to the following: The American Memory Project, Thomas Legislative Information, Congress at Work, Exhibitions an Online Gallery, Copyright Office and The Library Today. The American Memory project is an extensive and growing collection of digitized historical resources such as Federal Theater Project, Historic American Sheet Music, Historic Baseball Cards and Walt Whitman's Notebooks. (Note: Thomas Legislative Information is described in the "United States: Federal Government" section of this guide.)

**Authority:** U.S. Library of Congress

## Libweb: Library Servers via WWW

http://sunsite.berkeley.edu/Libweb/

An astonishing number of library websites are in this index. At the time of printing, it listed more than 6,100 pages from Academic, Public, National, Regional, State, Special and School libraries in more than 100 countries. Search by keyword or browse the regional alphabetic lists to find specific libraries.

**Authority:** Thomas Dowling, University of California, Berkeley

## National Library Catalogues Worldwide

http://www.library.uq.edu.au/natlibs/

Many countries have national libraries like the Library of Congress. This site is an index of those that have an Internet presence. Most of these catalogs are available via telnet, so a user or log-in name and exit command are needed. These requirements are listed along with the name of the library.

**Authority:** Library, University of Queensland

# Library Associations (*see also*

Associations)

**Note:** This is a selected list of library related associations. For a larger more comprehensive list, visit AcqWeb at http://www.library.vanderbilt.edu/law/acqs/acqs.html

## American Association of School Librarians

http://www.ala.org/aasl/

AASL is a division of the American Library Association and is included on the ALA page. However, this link goes directly to the AASL main page. This page includes information specific to the American Association of School Librarians and is organized into the following areas: About AASL, Awards, Grants & Scholarships, Career Development & Continuing Education, National Guidelines & Standards, Position Statements, Publications & Journals, Resource Guides, Technology and The AASL Community. The site is keyword-searchable and contains a site map of the page contents.

**Authority:** American Association of School Librarians

## American Library Association

http://www.ala.org/

This official site includes all kinds of information relating to the library profession. It is divided into the following areas: News and Announcements, Events and Conferences, Library Advocacy and Support, Education and Employment, Awards, ALA Interests and Activities, The Marketplace, Membership Info and Services, ALA's Library and ALA Divisions, Units, Governance. To make finding specific information easier, a comprehensive site map is available as is a search engine.

**Authority:** American Library Association

## Internet Library Association

http://www-org.usm.edu/~ila/

Although this newcomer to the world of library associations shows promise, the site doesn't seem to be updated very often. ILA was incorporated in 1996, and membership is free. "The mission of the Internet Library Association to educate, inform, support and unite librarians and information specialists world-wide on the Internet." This site has divided its content into five broad areas including: About ILA, ILA News, Internet News, Library Links and How-To Guides.

**Authority:** Internet Library Association

## Public Library Association

http://www.pla.org/

A division of the American Library Association, the PLA "exists to provide a diverse program of communi-cation, publication, advocacy, continuing education and programming for its members and others interested in the advancement of public library service." This site is divided into several areas including: Welcome to PLA, Continuing Education, Publications, Awards and Grants, News from PLA and Internet Resources.

**Authority:** Public Library Association

## Research Libraries Group

http://www.rlg.org/

"RLG is a not-for-profit membership corporation of over 160 universities, national libraries, archives, historical societies and other institutions with remarkable collections for research and learning. Rooted in collaborative work that addresses members' shared goals for these collections, RLG develops and operates information resources used by members and non-members around the world." It is divided into the following sections: What's New, RLG and You, Member Activities, User Resources & Services and Electronic & Print Publications. The site is keyword-searchable, though many if not all of the resources created by the RLG require subscriptions.

**Authority:** Research Libraries Group

## Society of American Archivists

http://www.archivists.org/

The mission statement reads: "the Society of American Archivists serves the educational and informational needs of its members and provides leadership to help ensure the identification, preservation and use of the nation's historical record." The opening page lists "Hot Topics" in the central area and on the right is a menu bar of items grouped into three broad areas: Products & Services, Groups and About SAA. The site is keyword-searchable.

**Authority:** Society of American Archivists

## Special Libraries Association

http://www.sla.org/

Special libraries can be found everywhere. Most frequently they are located in private businesses, public corporations, government agencies and hospitals. The central part of the page contains announcements and news related to the field. The left side menu bar includes sections such as Events, Conferences & Exhibits, Shop at SLA, Learn with SLA and Virtual Community. The site is keyword-searchable.

**Authority:** Special Libraries Association

# Magazines and Journals

## BUBL Journals

http://bubl.ac.uk/journals/

BUBL includes the "abstracts or full texts of over 200 current journals and newsletters. Coverage goes back to 1992 or 1993, though a few go back even further and some have been introduced more recently." Journals that are no longer available are part of the archive. The site is keyword-searchable. There is an alphabetic list of journal titles and several subject categories.

**Authority:** BUBL Information Service andersonian Library, Strathclyde University

## Editor and Publisher Media Links

http://emedia1.mediainfo.com/emedia/

Here is a site which is trying to bring all forms of electronic media to one searchable site. Keyword searching is one method for finding resources in this database. Another method is to browse by geographic location or by media type. Types of media include Associations, City Guides, Magazines, Newspapers, Radio, Syndicates/News Services and Television.

**Authority:** Editor & Publisher Co.

## Education Resources Information Clearinghouse: ERIC

http://www.eric.ed.gov/searchdb/dbchart_s.html

ERIC is one of the largest providers of access to journal articles and documents on education. This site provides links to four different methods for accessing the ERIC database via the Internet. The differences among the four methods are listed in a single table making this resource the best place to begin searching ERIC.

**Authority:** Education Resources Information Clearinghouse

## E-Journals.Org

http://www.e-journals.org/

E-Journals.Org is part of the World Wide Web Virtual Library. An interesting and eclectic list of topics ranging from Buddhism to Telecoms provides access to the many e-journals indexed on the site.

**Authority:** Unknown, World Wide Web Virtual Library has endorsed the site.

## Electronic Journal Miner

http://ejournal.coalliance.org/

This grant-funded site takes a more scholarly approach to serials and the Internet. It has assigned Library of Congress Subject Headings to the serials (journals, magazines and newsletters). The database is browsable by Library of Congress Subject Heading or by title. It is also keyword-searchable. This site does not search for articles within periodicals.

**Authority:** Colorado Alliance of Research Libraries

## Ingenta

http://www.ingenta.com/

The Ingenta database includes over 26,000 periodicals and more than 11,500,000 articles. Coverage of each magazine or journal title varies but most have been indexed since 1988. There is a "pay for" document delivery service built into Ingenta. However, the database is searchable for free. Search it by keyword, author, name or journal title. Entries include bibliographic citation and brief abstract.

**Authority:** Ingenta

## IPL Online Serials

http://www.ipl.org/reading/serials/

The Internet Public Library has organized more than 3,000 serial titles into broad subject areas such as Arts & Humanities, Business & Economics, Education, Science & Technology and Social Sciences. It is keyword-searchable or can be browsed by subject or title.

**Authority:** Internet Public Library

## PubList

http://www.publist.com/

PubList contains bibliographic data for more than 150,000 periodicals. The database is searchable by title keyword. The custom search feature allows searching by publisher, ISSN and/or description. The site includes browsable subject, title and publisher lists. The database entries include the title, ISSN, status, frequency of publication, special features, publisher address, publisher website, publisher fax, publisher e-mail and editor's name. This is not a source for articles in journals or magazines.

**Authority:** Bowes & Associates, Inc., Ulrich's International Periodicals Directory and Editor & Publisher International Yearbook

## University of Houston Libraries' Indexes, Abstracts, Bibliographies and Table of Contents Services

http://info.lib.uh.edu/indexes/indexes.htm

The goal here is to "provide access to indexes, abstracts, bibliographies and table of contents services that will help you find journal, magazine and newspaper articles, research papers, preprints, proceedings and transactions, book chapters and similar materials." This site is arranged first into three broad subject headings: Art & Humanities, Sciences & Technology and Social Sciences and then by narrower subjects groupings. It has not been updated since 1998. Currently it appears to have many more functioning links than dead ones.

**Authority:** Nancy Buchanan, Librarian and Jennifer Atkinson Librarian, University of Houston

## Mailing Lists

### CataList

http://www.lsoft.com/catalist.html

CataList is the official catalog of LISTSERV lists. Listserv is a mailing list software program. Currently there are more than 50,000 public Listserv mailing lists in the database. The site is keyword-searchable or browsable by geographic region.

**Authority:** L-Soft international, Inc.

### PAML The Directory of Publicly Accessible Mailing Lists

http://www.paml.net/

One of the oldest directories of mailing lists on the Web, this site was started in 1981. According to the introduction: "We might not be the biggest, but we personally guarantee that our listings are the most accurate." There are both name and subject indexes to browse through along with a search option.

**Authority:** Stephanie and Peter da Silva

### Tile.net

http://www.tile.net/

This site includes a searchable database of mailing lists, Usenet newsgroups and FTP sites. Searches can be restricted to a type of resource like FTP or on all available records in the database.

**Authority:** List-Universe.com

### Topica

http://www.topica.com/

Topica is similar to Yahoo Groups in that it provides hosting to thousands of mailing lists. It is browsable by subject or searchable by keyword.

**Authority:** Topica Inc.

### Yahoo Groups

http://groups.yahoo.com/

There are thousands of mailing lists on this site. You can find a mailing list to join by browsing through the subject categories or searching by keyword. Yahoo also allows individuals and organizations to create their own mailing lists.

**Authority:** Yahoo! Inc.

## Mathematics *(see also* Measurements; Science; Statistics*)*

### A + Math

http://www.aplusmath.com/

This easy-to-use site is designed to "help students improve their math skills interactively." It has four main sections: Flashcards, Game Room, Homework Helper and Worksheets. Within the sections are games and activities on mathematical topics such as Addition, Multiplication, Geometry, Algebra and Money. (Grades K–12)

**Authority:** Aplusmath.com

### Ask Dr. Math

http://forum.swarthmore.edu/dr.math/dr-math.html

An amazing site which allows students to "submit questions to Dr. Math by filling out our Web form or by sending in e-mail. Answers are sent back by e-mail and we then gather these questions and answers into a searchable archive organized by grade level (elementary, middle school, high school) and topic (exponents, infinity, polynomials, etc.)." The site is keyword-searchable. (Grades K–Undergraduate)

**Authority:** The Math Forum

### Coolmath4kids

http://www.coolmath4kids.com/

"An amusement park of math" is an apt description of this colorful site. The learning activities, lessons, puzzles, games and tests are arranged into categories such as Math Games, Jigsaw Puzzles, Coloring Books and Brain Benders. There are links to related sites for kids 13–100 and a special areas for teachers and parents. The site does not include a search engine. (Grades K–12)

**Authority:** Karen (M.S. in Mathematics) and Coolmath.com, Inc.

### Flashcards for Kids

http://www.edu4kids.com/math/

This site generates online flashcards for addition, subtraction, multiplication and division. There are many options for customization. For example you can choose easy, simple or hard from the complexity column and you can choose to run a timer or not. (Grades 1–8)

**Authority:** CANITech

### MacTutor History of Mathematics Archive

http://www-groups.dcs.st-andrews.ac.uk/~history/

The information on this site can be accessed from any of the following indexes: Biographies Index (1300+ individual biographies), History Topics Index (30 topical articles) and Famous curves index (60 curves with their history & properties). Alternately you can use the keyword search box to find a specific biography or article. Each biographical entry includes factual information, references, quotations and a brief biography. The Mathematicians of the Day area lists mathematicians who were born/died on this day in history.

**Authority:** John J O'Connor and Edmund F Robertson, School of Mathematical and Computational Sciences, University of St Andrews

### Math Forum @ Drexel

http://mathforum.org/

There are four main sections on this site: Student Center, Teachers' Place, Research Division and Parents & Citizens. Other sections that are available include What's New, Forum Features, Math Resources by Subject, Math Education and Key Issues in Math. From the main four you can access a wealth of information, problems, activities and lesson plans. Ask Dr. Math is sponsored on this site. (Grades K–Undergraduate) ✎

**Authority:** The Math Forum of Drexel University

### Math2.org

http://www.math2.org/index.xml

This helpful site contains all kinds of math tables. The tables are organized by subject and include: General Math, Algebra, Geometry, Trigonometry, Statistics, Calculus and Advanced Topics. Links to other related sites are included. (Grades 4–Undergraduate)

**Authority:** David Manura

### Mathematical Atlas

http://www.math.niu.edu/~rusin/known-math/welcome.html

Billed as "a gateway to Mathematics" this site is a valuable index to advanced mathematical topics on the Web. It is a "collection of short articles designed to provide an introduction to the areas of modern mathematics and pointers to further information, as well as answers to some common (or not!) questions." Arranged under broad topics that range from Combinatorics to Probability and Statistics are essays, links, bibliographic citations, problems, solutions and

embedded relational links. The site is keyword-searchable. (Undergraduate–Graduate) ∞

**Authority:** Dave Rusin, Associate Professor, Dept. of Mathematical Sciences, Northern Illinois University

### Mathematics of Cartography

http://math.rice.edu/~lanius/pres/map/

This site discusses math and maps at length. The main section headings are in the form of questions and include: What exactly are maps? What is the history of mapmaking? What mathematics do you use with maps? and Want to solve some problems? Lists of resources, both on- and offline and teacher notes are also available.

**Authority:** Cynthia Lanius, Center for Center for Excellence and Equity in Education, Rice University

### Mathmania

http://www.theory.csc.uvic.ca/~mmania/

Mathmania contains all kinds of math information including stories, activities, tutorials and exercises. Its goal is to help young students explore topics in higher mathematics. Although the topics seem to be aimed at high schoolers, this page has a lot of activities that can be adopted for grades K–8. (Grades K–12)

**Authority:** Mathmania

### What Good is Math?

http://www.richmond.edu/~ed344/webunits/math/home.htm

This creative site uses topics like planning a party, various sports and shopping to show how math can be used in real life situations. A nice site for helping students understand the value of mathematics. (Grades K–12)

**Authority:** Jen Peck, Karen Rosser, Carol Pifer, Mary Beth Indelicato and Dr. Patricia Stohr-Hunt, University of Richmond

## Measurements (*see also* Mathematics; Science)

### Dictionary of Units

http://www.ex.ac.uk/cimt/dictunit/dictunit.htm

This site "provides a summary of most of the units of measurement to be found in use around the world today (and a few of historical interest), together with the appropriate conversion factors needed to change them into a 'standard' unit of the S I [Systeme

International]." It is arranged by category such as Volume, Viscosity, Torque, Area and Speed. Many of the sections include forms for conversion.

**Authority:** Frank Tapson, Centre for Innovation in Mathematics Teaching, University of Exeter.

## How Many? A Dictionary of Units of Measurement

http://www.unc.edu/~rowlett/units/

This dictionary includes all kinds of measurement definitions. It is arranged in alphabetical order by name of measurement. The letter H section includes definitions for terms such as Hank, Hat Size, Heat Index, Heer and Hubble. The site also includes articles about various measurements and links to related web pages.

**Authority:** Russ Rowlett, Director, Center for Mathematics and Science Education, University of North Carolina, Chapel Hill

## Measure 4 Measure

http://www.wolinskyweb.com/measure.htm

The links on this multifaceted site lead to other web pages that have interactive calculators. These interactive calculators or programs can measure, estimate and figure. Scroll down the site to browse through the measurement categories which include: Science/Math, Health, Finance and A Measure of Everything Else. ∞

**Authority:** Measure 4 Measure

## World Wide Metric Calculators

http://www.worldwidemetric.com/metcal.htm

This calculator can convert length, weight, pressure and volume into metric measurements.

**Authority:** Robert Collette for World Wide Metric Co. Inc.

# Movies (*see also* Biography; Drama; Prizes and Awards)

## Hollywood Online

http://www.hollywood.com/

A complicated site, Hollywood.com contains "over one million pages of in-depth movie information, including movie descriptions and reviews, showtime listings, entertainment news and an extensive multimedia library." The advanced search engine has the ability to limit in various ways. The limits are grouped under the categories: Celebrities, Movies, Multimedia, News and Features.

**Authority:** Hollywood Online Inc.

## Internet Movie Database

http://www.imdb.com/

The IMDB is probably the biggest and most comprehensive database of movie and television information on the Web. Filmographies listing an actors work noting every movie role and most television appearances are available. If an actor has also done directing or producing those films will also be listed. Search the site by keyword, people, characters or title. Entries include biographical information, reviews and plot summaries.

**Authority:** The Internet Movie Database Ltd.

## Movie Review Query Engine (MRQE)

http://www.mrqe.com/

MRQE indexes more than 200,000 movie reviews. For instance the first Jurassic Park movie has links to 77 different reviews including the Chicago Sun-Times (Roger Ebert) and Rolling Stone. The site is searchable by movie title. An advanced search engine allows the use of and or and adj. ∞

**Authority:** Stewart M. Clamen

## Mr. Showbiz

http://mrshowbiz.go.com/

Hundreds of reviews and articles and basic movie information are available on this site. The main contents are divided into the following sections: News, Celebrities, Movies and DVDs. The site is keyword-searchable.

**Authority:** Mr. Showbiz

## Upcomingmovies.com

http://www.upcomingmovies.com/

Upcomingmovies.com, "where you can find out about tomorrow's movies today. This site provides previews of the movies heading our way in the coming months. Each preview gives cast, crew and plot information and includes my commentary and thoughts on what the movie might be like." This site is searchable alphabetically by title, expected release date or by name (actor, writer, director).

**Authority:** Greg Dean Schmitz

# Museums (*see also* Art; Architecture; Drama)

## Museumstuff.com

http://museumstuff.com/

This is a guide to museum websites and museum related information from around the world. There are over 8,000 "museum related" links included in the keyword-searchable index. There are four main subject sections on the first page including: Art & Design, History & Culture, Science & Tech. and Miscellaneous.

**Authority:** MuseumStuff.com and Discovery Media

### WWW Virtual Library: Museums Around the World

http://vlmp.museophile.com/world.html

"This page includes an eclectic collection of World Wide Web services connected with museums around the world." It is organized by country then in alphabetical order by name of museum.

**Authority:** Jonathan Bowen

### WWW Virtual Library: Museums in the USA

http://www.museumca.org/usa/

Hundreds of museums are currently indexed by this site. All are located in the U.S.A. and have Web pages. All kinds of museums are represented, including art, children, history, science, technology, multi-disciplinary and miscellaneous. The database can be searched by museum name, subject or keyword. The site also provides lists of museums by name, state or type.

**Authority:** John Burke, Chief Conservator, Oakland Museum

# Music (*see also* Drama; Prizes and Awards)

### CD Connection

http://www.cdconnection.com/

The largest number of search options can be found on this commercial music site. From the pull-down menu at the top of the page you can search by popular artist, cd/soundtrack title, song title, classical performer, classical orchestra, classical composer, classical work, manufacturers' label, manufacturer's catalog number, CDC part number or "any field containing...." This is a fairly straightforward site, as it provides recommendations, but gives little else in the way of extra information. While it does not have a "browsable by genre" option it does include a source for rare items.

**Authority:** CD Connection and Muze

### CD Universe

http://www.cduniverse.com

The commercial CD Universe is searchable by artist, title, song, soundtrack and label. There are many "sound samples" in the database. A "sound sample" is

a piece of song in an audio file format. The site also sells games and movies.

**Authority:** CD Universe

### CDnow

http://www.cdnow.com/

This commercial music site is searchable by artist, title, song title, record label and soundtrack. Each artist in the database has a discography page, a biography page and a list of web links. Web links or biography pages may be blank in some cases.

**Authority:** CDnow, Inc.

### Classical Composers Database

http://utopia.knoware.nl/users/jsmeets/abc.htm

More than 1,500 entries are arranged into an alphabetical list of composer last names. Each entry includes the following information: born, died, music, life and links. Most of the information in these sections are sketchy at best or missing altogether for some composers. But the links can be valuable and the site is definitely growing and improving.

**Authority:** Jos Smeets

### DigiTrad Lyrics Database

http://www.mudcat.org

The Mudcat Cafe hosts a database of traditional folk song lyrics. Many of the entries include playable audio files. Use the DigiTrad Lyrics Search box in the upper left quadrant to find songs by keyword or use the clickable alphabet in the bottom of the same box to browse the list of songs. "Lyrics, Forum & Chat."

**Authority:** Mudcat Cafe, Music Foundation, Inc.

### Instrument Encyclopedia

http://www.si.umich.edu/chico/instrument/

Information on this site is accessible in three major ways. First is via a browse where you can browse the general reference information, the classification listings or country of origin. Second is via a search form and third is through a set of pages set up for educators. The entries are several paragraphs in length and include illustrations.

**Authority:** School of Information and School of Music, University of Michigan

### K–12 Resources for Music Educators

http://www.isd77.k12.mn.us/resources/staffpages/ shirk/k12.music.html

This handy site indexes websites for music teachers. It is arranged into the following lists: Sites For Band

Teachers, Sites For Orchestra Teachers, Sites For Vocal/Choral Teachers, Sites For Classroom Music Teachers, Valuable Sites For All Music Educators, Links to Commercial Music Resources, Links to Biographies and Works of the Great Composers, Music Search Engines, Still More Music Links!, Link to MIDI Resources and Link to Music Newsgroups.  ∞

**Authority:** Cynthia Mazurkiewicz Shirk

## Music for the Nation: American Sheet Music, 1870–1885

http://memory.loc.gov/ammem/smhtml/smhome.html

Part of the American Memory Collection sponsored by the Library of Congress, this priceless site consists of more than 45,000 full-image pieces of sheet music. Included are popular songs, piano music, sacred music, secular choral music, solo instrumental music, method books, instructional materials and music for band and orchestra. A catalog record and a complete digital copy of the work is available for each piece of sheet music. Search the site by author, title, subject or keyword.

**Authority:** U.S. Library of Congress

## Musicsearch.com

http://musicsearch.com

Since 1996 MusicSearch has been indexing music-related websites. Search the database of over 20,000 reviewed links by keyword. You can also use the meta search function to search other music related directories and websites.

**Authority:** MusicSearch

## Mutopia

http://www.mutopiaproject.org/

Mutopia is a full text resource for musical scores. The site has been compiled by volunteers and "is similar in spirit to Project Gutenburg." There are hundreds of compositions in the database. You can find a work by keyword searching or by browsing through the lists of composers, instruments or musical styles.

**Authority:** Chris Sawer

## Pepper Music Network

http://jwpepper.com

In business since 1845, this site is billed as the "World's Largest Sheet Music Retailer." The online catalog is both keyword-searchable and genre-browsable.

**Authority:** J.W. Pepper & Son, Inc.

## Sibelius Academy Music Resources

http://www.siba.fi/kulttuuripalvelut/music.html

An extensive index to music websites on the Internet, this site was awarded PC Magazine's Top 100 status in 1996. It is organized in broad categories such as Opera, Early Music and Music Magazines.  ∞

**Authority:** Sibelius Academy

# Mythology (*see also* Full-Text Resources; History; Reading and Literature)

## Bulfinch's Mythology

http://www.bulfinch.org/

This is a full-text version of the classic *Bulfinch's Mythology*. The site is divided into three sections: Age of Fable, Age of Chivalry and Legends of Charlemagne. The contents are cross-referenced with many hypertext links to related websites and material.

**Authority:** Thomas Bulfinch and Bob Fisher

## Encyclopedia Mythica

http://pantheon.org/mythica/

Over 5,700 "definitions of gods and goddesses, supernatural beings and legendary creatures and monsters from all over the world" are included in this site. Browse through the encyclopedia by selecting a culture or search by keyword.

**Authority:** Encyclopedia Mythica and M.F. Lindemans

## Folklore and Mythology Electronic Texts

http://www.pitt.edu/~dash/folktexts.html

The full-text of hundreds of tales are included on this website. There are two pages arranged in alphabetical order by topic. A page of related links and a special section on Germanic Myths, Legends and Sagas are included. As for the legends themselves, they range from the familiar such as "The Emperor's New Clothes" to the obscure such as "Ertha, the Germanic Earth Goddess."

**Authority:** Professor D. L. Ashliman, University of Pittsburgh

## Greek Mythology Link

http://hsa.brown.edu/~maicar/

This award-winning site is based on the book *Genealogical Guide to Greek Mythology* by Carlos Parada, who is also the author of this website. All of the entries are based "on original sources, that is, authors from the period between approximately 800 BC and AD 600." All kinds of articles can be found here, topics include: genealogy, relationships, history and abbreviated stories about the gods, goddesses and characters in Greek Mythology. Search for entries by keyword or look through lists such as Dieties, Biographies, Maps, Peoples and Places and Catalogue of Images.

**Authority:** Carlos Parada

## Legends

http://www.legends.dm.net/

Legends promises to access primary sources when available, provide personal essays and extended reviews and give historical surveys and thoughtful commentary. Topics on this site include: The Robin Hood Pages, King Arthur & the Matter of Britain, Ballads & Broadsides, Pirates & Privateers, Swashbucklers & Fops, Erin & Alba, Fairy Tales, Shakespeare's Stories, Beowulf, Sagas & Sea-Kings, Paladins & Princes, Poets & Painters and Legendary Resources. Links to full-text resources on the topic are available on each entry as are links to other related sites. The site is keyword-searchable. ∞

**Authority:** Dueling Modems

## Mythology and Folklore

http://www.pibburns.com/mythfolk.htm

This is an extensive index to mythology and folklore related websites. It is arranged into four main categories. 1. General Folklore and Mythology Sites "offers links to sites with miscellaneous information about folklore or mythology. Includes a number of excellent index sites as well as sites for story-tellers." 2. Journals, Mailing Lists, Newsgroups, Societies and University Departments "lists a variety of print and electronic publications about mythology and folklore. It also offers links to societies, university departments and USENET newsgroups." 3. Regional Folklore and Mythology "offers folklore, myths and legends organized by cultural and geographical region." 4. Special Topics in Folklore and Mythology "offers information about astronomical and meteorological myths and legends (including global flood myths), urban legends, Mithraism, Cinderella and Grimm's Fairy Tales." The only thing this site lacks is a search engine. ∞

**Authority:** Philip R. "Pib" Burns

# Newsgroups

## Google Groups

http://groups.google.com/

In 2001 the search engine Google acquired Deja.com and the contents of the archived Usenet groups. The keyword-searchable archives begin in 1995. Alternately you can use the advance search to narrow by forum, message, subject, author, language, topic or dates. There is also an arranged content directory of the content.

**Authority:** Deja News

## Internet FAQ Archives

http://www.faqs.org/faqs/

An amazing number of FAQ (Frequently Asked Questions) lists have been produced by the numerous Usenet groups on the Internet. FAQs contain quality information related to the topic of the Usenet forum. This archive indexes by hierarchy, category and name and searches the FAQs.

**Authority:** FAQS.org

# Newspapers

## AJR Newslink

http://ajr.newslink.org/

A great resource for current events, an impressive 18,000 newspaper and news media sites are gathered into this database. Select from four main sections: Sites, Articles, Interact and Special. Use the search feature in the Interact section to search by title, name or keyword.

**Authority:** American Journalism Review Magazine and NewsLink Associates

## IPL Reading Room: Online Newspapers

http://www.ipl.org/reading/news/

The Internet Public Library has collected URLs for hundreds of national and international newspapers. The site is organized by country of origin and then alphabetically by newspaper title. ∞

**Authority:** Internet Public Library

## NewsDirectory.Com

http://www.ecola.com/archive/press/

There are more than 14,500 links in the NewsDirectory index. The links go to each newspaper's searchable archive or search engine. The NewsDirectory service has been available online since 1995. ∞

**Authority:** NewsDirectory.com

## News Index

http://www.newsindex.com/

News Index provides access to current news information. To access the full-text of a news story, search by keyword or click on any of the headlines listed on the page. Over 300 newspapers and other news sources are included in the index.

**Authority:** News Index

## U.S. News Archives on the Web

http://www.ibiblio.org/riverat/internet/archives.html

This site indexes only U.S. newspapers. The entries are arranged geographically by state then by city and paper and include links to the paper and the paper's archives. Entries also include a date when the archives started and costs for full-text retrieval of articles. A link to non-U.S. newspaper archives is located in the introductory material on the first page. ⚭

**Authority:** News Division Volunteers of the Special Libraries Association

# Nutrition (*see also* Health and Medicine)

## Food Finder

http://www.olen.com/food/

This cool site gives nutritional information on the items sold by fast food places like KFC, White Castle, Taco Bell, McDonald's and Pizza Hut. It is a great way to get children interested in nutrition. Calories, fat, calories from fat, cholesterol, sodium, carbohydrates, protein, fiber and sugars are listed for most menu items.

**Authority:** Minnesota Attorney General's Office and Olen Publishing

## Nutrition.Gov

http://www.nutrition.gov/

"This national resource makes obtaining government information on nutrition, healthy eating, physical activity and food safety, easily accessible in one place for many Americans." There is information on topics ranging from food assistance programs to the food pyramid. To find articles, graphics and other resources you can either browse by category or search by keyword.

**Authority:** Nutrition.Gov, U.S. Federal Government

## Tufts University Nutrition Navigator

http://navigator.tufts.edu/

This solid site has been designed to solve two problems: how to find good information and whether or not to trust the information. The database consists of nutritionist-evaluated sites. Each entry has been rated and given a review. The site can be searched or browsed using the following categories: Kids, Women, Parents, General Nutrition, Journalists, Health Professionals, Educators and Special Dietary Needs.

**Authority:** Center of Nutrition Communication, School of Nutrition Science and Policy, Tufts University.

## USDA Center for Nutrition Policy Promotion

http://www.usda.gov/cnpp/

"The Center for Nutrition Policy and Promotion was created in the U.S. Department of Agriculture, December 1, 1994 and is the focal point within USDA where scientific research is linked with the nutritional needs of the American public." The links on this page lead to articles, guidelines and "Using the Food Guide Pyramid: A Resource for Nutrition Educators," a .pdf formatted guide to teaching nutrition. There are also links to other Food and Nutrition-related government sites.

**Authority:** Center for Nutrition Policy and Promotion

# Optical Illusions (*see also* Art; Physics and Astronomy)

## IllusionWorks

http://www.illusionworks.com/

All kinds of optical illusions are explained and illustrated on this award-winning site. The page is divided into sections including: Introduction to Illusions, Interactive Demonstrations, Illusions in Art, Illusion Puzzles and 3-D Illusions. A list of related links is also provided.

**Authority:** IllusionWorks, LLC

## SandlotScience.com: Optical Illusions

http://www.sandlotscience.com/index.htm

This amazing optical illusion site includes: demonstrations, artwork, animation, stories, projects, games and puzzles. These items are divided into 10 categories such as impossible objects, typography and ambiguous figures.

**Authority:** SandlotScience

# Paleontology

## Dino Russ's Lair

http://www.isgs.uiuc.edu/dinos/dinos_home.html

The primary purpose of this site "is to promote information about dinosaurs and vertebrate paleontology." There are literally hundreds of websites indexed on this page. They are grouped into categories such as Dinosaur

Sites to Visit, Tracks and Dinosaur Information. The Dinosaur Information section is subdivided into the following sections: Dinosaur Courses and Educational Materials Online, For Younger Children, General Information Sites, Regional Information, Specific Dinosaurs or Dinosaur groups and Top References. (Grades K–Graduate) ∞ ✎

**Authority:** Russell J. Jacobson, Illinois State Geological Survey

### Dinosaur Links

http://www.ucmp.berkeley.edu/diapsids/dinolinks.html

All things dinosaur are collected in this link site. There are seven main categories to choose from including: Dinosaur-Oriented Sites, Dinosaurs & Paleontology, Dinosaurs in Museums organizations & Institutions, Dinosaur Art & Models, Dinosaurs as Movie Stars, Not Dinosaurs but Worthy of Mention. A list of dinosaur websites for kids can be found in the first section. (Grades K–Undergraduate) ∞

**Authority:** John R. Hutchinson, Dept. of Integrative Biology, University of California, Berkeley

### Dinosauricon

http://dinosauricon.com/

This site includes "a gallery of images from many talented artists, a variety of fact-filled charts on things dinosaurian. And details on every single species of non-avian dinosaur." The site is arranged in the following sections: Introduction, Art Gallery, Guest Book, Finding Information, Special Topics, Features and Other Sources. Use the Genus list to access the dinosaur information and be sure to scroll down the page. A typical entry contains information about the dinosaur's measurements, place in time, location or place, type of remains and images.

**Authority:** T. Michael Keesey

### Museum of Paleontology

http://www.ucmp.berkeley.edu/

This site has so many resources it would be difficult to describe them all. Many different kinds of fossils are represented including invertebrates, vertebrates and paleobotanicals. Pictures, articles, links, charts and other information are available. Click on "Discover the History of Life" to access exhibits and activities. Alternately you can go directly to the Web-based educational models at: http://www.ucmp.berkeley.edu/ education/explotime.html. The entire museum site is keyword-searchable. (Grades 6–12) ✎

**Authority:** University of California, Berkeley

### Plant Fossil Record

http://ibs.uel.ac.uk/palaeo/pfr2/pfr.htm

The "database includes descriptions and occurrences of many thousands of extinct plants. For the first time modern genera with fossil species are included in the description database." The database is divided into the following searchable categories: Genera, Descriptions, Taxonomy, Occurrences and Paleo Maps.

**Authority:** International Organization of Paleobotany

# Patents (*see also* Business and Economics)

### Delphion Intellectual Property Network

http://www.delphion.com/

Formerly the IBM Intellectual Property Network, this site has three different access levels. The first is free and includes access to U.S. bibliographic patent data. The full-text of the patents can be purchased.

**Authority:** U.S. Patent & Trademark Office and Delphion Intellectual Property

### QPAT-US

http://www.qpat.com

QPAT is a commercial front end to the U.S. Patent and Trademark Database. The site information states that it offers "revolutionary ease of use and power to the patent searcher." It offers free access to abstracts of patent records filed since 1974. Registration is required to use any part of this database. Full-text is available for a fee. The USPTO Web Patent Databases offers the full-text for free and doesn't require registration. However, locating patent information can sometimes be difficult. Since all of the patent sites access the database differently, all can be useful when searching for patents.

**Authority:** U.S. Patent & Trademark Office and QPAT

### USPTO Web Patent Databases

http://www.uspto.gov/patft/index.html

This site has access to three databases. The U.S. Patent Grants Database contains the full-text since 1976 and the full-page images since 1790. A second database on the page includes past few months of Patent Applications. The contents of both are searchable by Patent Classification.

**Authority:** U.S. Patent & Trademark Office

# Philosophy *(see also* Full Text Resources; Religion; Social Studies)

### EpistemeLinks

http://www.epistemelinks.com/

Thousands of philosophy-related websites are indexed here. The page is divided into many sections including: Philosophers, Topics, E-Texts, Images, Classroom, Journals, Newsgroups, Fun and Humor and Other Link Sites. The site is keyword-searchable. ∞

**Authority:** Thomas Ryan Stone

### Internet Encyclopedia of Philosophy

http://www.utm.edu/research/iep/

A well-organized site which has an extremely useful timeline of articles on movements and philosophers. There is a short, alphabetically arranged list of full-text philosophy sources. A keyword index makes searching a lot easier. Alternately, click on the alphabet at the top of the page to browse through the encyclopedia. Articles are adapted from the public domain, from material written by the site editor or are contributions from professional philosophers.

**Authority:** Dr. James Fieser and Dr. Bradley Dowden, University of Tennessee, Martin

### Noesis: Philosophical Research On-Line

http://noesis.evansville.edu/bin/index.cgi

Noesis "is an indexing and accrediting effort dedicated to organizing the philosophical content of the Internet into an academically viable network of resources for use by philosophy teachers, researchers and students." It indexes "meaningful" self-publication, online journals in philosophy and two encyclopedias. The site is browsable by author, collection or topic. It is also searchable.

**Authority:** Internet Applications Laboratory, University of Evansville

### Philosophers: Alphabetical Index

http://users.ox.ac.uk/~worc0337/philosophers.html

The simple arrangement of this site makes it very easy to use. Scroll down the alphabetical list to the correct last name. Then, click through to a page of related websites. There is a chronological index and a list of related websites.

**Authority:** Dr Peter J. King

### Stanford Encyclopedia of Philosophy

http://plato.stanford.edu/contents.html

Stanford produces this valuable encyclopedia. The encyclopedia is dynamic in that new articles are con-stantly being added and older articles maintained and improved. Articles include topics such as "Aristotle's Political Theory" and "The Nature of Law" are available. Look through the "What's New" list, browse the alphabetically arranged topics or search by keyword to find articles.

**Authority:** Metaphysics Research Lab, Center for the Study of Language and Information, Stanford University

# Phone Books

### AnyWho

http://www.anywho.com/

Yellow Pages, White Pages, Reverse Lookup, Toll Free and Websites are the names of the file tabs that appear on this site. A nice feature is the toll-free search engine. This toll-free database can be searched by name or state or city or browsed by subject listing.

**Authority:** AT&T

### International White and Yellow Pages

http://www.wayp.com/

An international index of white, yellow or fax directories, this site is useful for finding phone numbers from around the world. Access the directories by selecting the continent and country name. A list of international calling codes is included on the site. ∞

**Authority:** Wajens Internet Group

### PhoneNumbers.net

http://www.phonenumbers.net/

Start searching this site by choosing a country from the drop down menu or continent from the top menu options. There are four categories of directories listed: Phone-Residential, Phone, Business/Organization, E-mail Addresses and Miscellaneous. While the directories listed are not provided by this site, the links and organization make this page useful. ∞

**Authority:** AAU Aktiv IT AB

### Qwestdex.com

http://www.qwestdex.com/

More than just yellow pages can be found here. Business white pages, residential white pages, government and toll-free directories can be accessed. The database is searchable by name, category, address, city and state. Be sure to uncheck the "Surrounding Area" box if you wish to restrict your search to an exact city or town.

**Authority:** Qwest

### Telephone Directories on the Web

http://www.teldir.com/

Like many of the other telephone directory sites, this is also arranged first by continent and then by country. An attempt has been made to link to official telephone directories only, but selected business directories are included when no other telephone directory is available for a specific country. There are more than 400 directories to more than 170 countries on the website.

**Authority:** Infobel.com and Teldir.com

## Physical Education (*see also* Health and Medicine)

### PE Central

http://pe.central.vt.edu/

The site states that its goal is to "provide the latest information about contemporary developmentally appropriate physical education programs for children and youth." There are lesson plans, activities, instructional resources, links to other sites and professional information on this page. Lesson plans are reviewed by an editorial board before being posted. The site is keyword-searchable. (Grades PreK–12)

**Authority:** Mark Manross, Health and PE Program, Virginia Polytechnic Institute and State University

### Physical Education Lesson Plans

http://schools.eastnet.ecu.edu/pitt/ayden/physed.htm

Sponsored by the Ayden Elementary School, this site indexes more than 400 health/PE links and more than 120 lesson plans. The page was created mainly for K–4, but the lesson plans could be adapted for older kids. The links are organized into 15 categories, including Schools, Gymnastics and Adapted PhysEd. The Physical Education Lesson Plan section includes titles such as "Exercise Hunt," "Soft Lacrosse," and "Roll with It." There are also links to other physical education lesson plan sites. (Grades K–4)

**Authority:** John Williams, Physical Education Teacher, Ayden Elementary School

## Physics

### Amusement Park Physics

http://www.learner.org/exhibits/parkphysics/

A great site to help teach physics principles. Find out how various rides at amusement parks really work. This site includes the following rides: roller coaster, carousel, bumper cars, free fall and pendulum. The site is enriched by a basic physics glossary and related links.

**Authority:** Annenberg/CPB Project

### Energy Quest

http://www.energy.ca.gov/education/

A colorful site arranged into the areas such as: Watt's That, Ask Dr. Questor, Educational Resources, Energy Patrol and Science Projects. From these categories activities, lessons, articles and other websites can be accessed. (Grades K–12)

**Authority:** California Energy Commission.

### History of Physics Exhibits

http://www.aip.org/history/exhibit.htm

The mission of this site is "to preserve and make known the history of modern physics and allied fields including astronomy, geophysics, optics and the like." Currently there are six exhibits created by the American Institute of Physics including "The Discovery of the Electron" and "Albert Einstein: Image and Impact." Scroll down the page to access an enormous list of sites relating to the history of physics.

**Authority:** American Institute of Physics

### HyperPhysics

http://hyperphysics.phy-astr.gsu.edu/hphys.html

"HyperPhysics is a broad-ranging interactive physics exploration environment which is written in HTML with Javascript calculation routines," says the site. It has been designed to support a number of undergraduate physics courses. Use the image map of topics to access the graphics, definitions, activities and essays. Topics include Mechanics, Relativity, Quantum Physics and more. (Undergraduate)

**Authority:** Dr. Rod Nave, Dept. of Physics and Astronomy, Georgia State University

### Instructional Materials in Physics

http://www.cln.org/subjects/physics_inst.html

The sites included on this list "all have lesson plans/activities for the Physical Science classroom teacher." There are general resources on the first page and links to other subject lists for topics including Electricity, Kites, Magnetism, Paper Airplanes and Sound. (Grades K–12)

**Authority:** Open Learning Agency

## Physics 2000

http://www.Colorado.EDU/physics/2000/

The goals of the site include making physics more accessible to students and people of all ages, demonstrating the connection between modern technology and earlier basic research and fostering an appreciation of the accomplishments of 20th century physics. Cartoon characters and interactive animations are used throughout the site to explain different physics topics in a fun and nonthreatening manner. (Grades 7–Undergraduate)

**Authority:** Chemistry and Physics Depts. University of Colorado, Boulder

## PhysicsWeb

http://physicsweb.org/resources/

This Institute of Physics sponsored site has lists of information under the following headings: Educational, Media, Companies, Institutions & Organizations, Computing, Reference, Exhibitions & Museums, Other Resources and Miscellaneous. Click on any of these to view an annotated list of websites. Use the simple search box or click on "Advanced Search" at the top of the page to narrow your search by organization, country or field of interest. (High School–Undergraduate) ∞

**Authority:** Institute of Physics Publishing Ltd.

## PhysLink

http://www.physlink.com/

The stated mission of this site is "to provide comprehensive research and education tools to physicists, engineers, educators, students and all other curious minds." It provides comprehensive access to many physics resources including glossaries, periodic tables, news articles, software and activities. Use the search box, the category sections or the site map to find the resources. ∞

**Authority:** PhysLink.com

## Playground Physics

http://lyra.colorado.edu/sbo/mary/play/

Mary Urquhart has designed this page for teachers to use as an introduction to basic physics concepts. Currently there are three toys on the playground: Jungle-Gym Drop, See-Saw Physics and Swing Set Physics. (Grades 4–7)

**Authority:** Mary Urquhart

## The Soundry

http://library.thinkquest.org/19537/

From the site: "the Soundry is an exciting, interactive and educational website about sound. Covering everything from the most basic concepts of what sound actu-ally is to the specifics of how humans perceive it." The site is made of sections which include: The Ear, Physics, Applications, Timeline and Soundlab. Each section has a clickable table of contents to articles and images on the various topics. (Grades 7–Undergraduate)

**Authority:** Alex Kulesza, David Green and Granite Christopher

## University of Oregon Virtual Laboratory

http://jersey.uoregon.edu/vlab/

This is a collection of interactive Java applets to be used in teaching or studying physics, astronomy and environmental science. Right now the site has five sections including: Astrophysics, Energy & Environment, Mechanics, Thermodynamics and Tools. Each section has multiple Java tools listed such as "Motion in Two Dimensions—Cannon Challenge" and "Cosmology—Hubble Expansion Law."
(High School–Undergraduate)

**Authority:** David Mason, Amy McGrew, Sean Russell, David Caley and Dr. Greg Bothum, Dept.of Physics, University of Oregon

# Plagiarism (*see also Copyright*)

### Anti-Plagiarism

http://www.virtualsalt.com/antiplag.htm

This site consists of an essay on how to combat plagiarism of research papers. Topics covered in the essay include "why students cheat" and "use a plagiarism detector."

**Authority:** Robert Harris, author of *The Plagiarism Handbook*

### Cheating 101: Internet Paper Mills

http://www.coastal.edu/library/mills2.htm

A wonderful resource for finding websites that provide papers for students to download. It lists more than 150 general sites and many subject specific sites. ∞

**Authority:** Margaret Fain, Library Instruction Coordinator, Coastal Carolina University

### Plagiarism

http://www.indiana.edu/~wts/wts/plagiarism.html

The full title of this site reads: "Plagiarism: What It is and How to Recognize and Avoid It." It is a great guide for students and teachers who are concerned about plagiarism.

**Authority:** Writing Tutorial Services, Indiana University, Bloomington

### Plagiarism in Colleges

http://www.rbs2.com/plag.htm

"This essay discusses plagiarism from a legal perspective. For other perspectives on the problem of plagiarism, see the links section below." Links to related articles are embedded throughout the essay.

**Authority:** Dr. Ronald B. Standler, Attorney

### Plagiarism Theme Page

http://www.cln.org/themes/plagiarism.html

This is a web page of links to resources on Plagiarism. "Students and teachers will find curricular resources (information, content...) and reference materials to help them learn about this topic. In addition, there are also links to instructional materials (lesson plans) which will help teachers provide instruction in this theme." (Grades 5–Undergraduate)

**Authority:** Community Learning Network

### Plagiarized.com

http://www.plagiarized.com/

"The purpose of this site is to help teachers or professors (or even parents) determine if a given piece of academic work has been obtained from the Internet." It is divided into several sections including: Dead Giveaways, Online Training, Research, Advice, Articles and Copyright Info. The site is searchable via a box located on the bottom of the page.

**Authority:** Greggory Senechal, GSC Online

## Plug-ins

### Adobe Acrobat Reader

http://www.adobe.com/products/acrobat/readstep.html

Adobe Acrobat Reader is probably the most popular plug-in on the Web. It is required in order to read .pdf files. It is downloadable for free at this site.

**Authority:** Adobe Systems Inc.

### Browser Plug-ins

http://home.netscape.com/plugins/?cp=dowdep4

Netscape has created this page to facilitate the downloading of browser plug-ins. There are links to Apple QuickTime, Adobe Acrobat Reader, Macromedia Flash Player, Shockwave by Macromedia, RealPlayer by RealNetworks and Net2Phone. There is a link near the top of the page to check if you have the plug-ins already installed in Netscape. The links on the left side of the page take you to more information on plug-ins.

**Authority:** Netscape

### BrowserWatch—Plug-In Plaza

http://browserwatch.internet.com/plug-in.html

This is a "reference tool for locating the plug-ins you need. You can either browse through the comprehensive lists of plug-ins, arranged by category or zero in on the plug-in you want by using the lists arranged by platform below." There are more than 60 different plug-ins listed on the site. ∞

**Authority:** INT Media Group

### Plugins.com

http://www.plugins.com/

This resource for finding plug-ins is organized by browser list. There is a lot of advertising on this page so scroll down the page till you see "Select your poison!" and choose "Browser."

**Authority:** Cameron Gregory

## Prizes and Awards (see also Biography; Music; Reading and Literature)

### The Academy of Motion Picture Arts and Sciences (The Oscars)

http://www.oscars.org

The official site for the Oscars, this site has information about the Academy and what it does. Click on "Academy Awards" to information about the awards. Scroll to the bottom to access the Academy Awards database. It is a keyword-searchable index of winners since 1927. Other interesting links include History of the Academy Awards and About the Academy Awards.

**Authority:** Academy of Motion Picture Arts and Sciences

### Academy of Television Arts & Sciences (The Emmys)

http://www.emmys.org/

The official Emmy site includes information about the Academy and what it does. Click on "Emmy Awards" to access the database of nominees and winners since 1949. The site has other articles and information about both past and upcoming Award shows, lots of downloads and activities and information about the foundation.

**Authority:** Academy of Television Arts and Sciences

### Book Awards

http://www.literature-awards.com/

Click on the "Book Awards A–Z" link to access a directory of more than 100 book awards. Entries in the directory include the title, a brief description of the award, past and present winners and links to official award sites. There are special pages for the Nobel Prize and Pulitzer Prize. The site is keyword-searchable and alpha-browsable via the site map.

**Authority:** Jacqueline M. Lor

### Database of Award Winning Children's Literature

http://www2.wcoil.com/~ellerbee/childlit.html

A searchable database of award-winning juvenile literature. Age of reader, protagonist ethnicity, genre and historical period are some of the available search options. Reading lists can be generated from this database.

**Authority:** Lisa R. Bartle, Librarian, Ohio State University

### The National Academy of Recording Arts and Sciences (The Grammys)

http://www.grammy.com

The official Grammy site contains information, articles, photo gallery, calendar and more. Click on Winner's Search to access the database of winners since 1958. The site really needs a search engine or at the very least, a site map.

**Authority:** National Academy of Recording Arts and Sciences

### Nobel Foundation

http://www.nobel.se

This comprehensive site is arranged into the seven broad categories of Nobel, Physics, Chemistry, Medicine, Literature, Peace and Economics. Under each category are articles by and about the prize/winner. Entries can include pictures of the diplomas, links to other resources, speech transcripts, photographs of the ceremony and biographies. For the more recent winners the entries include video files. The database includes information on all winners since 1901.

**Authority:** The Nobel Foundation

### Pulitzer Prizes

http://www.pulitzer.org

This site includes a current winners list and a history of the prize. The centerpiece of the site is an archive of the full-text of many of the prize-winning works from 1995 to the present. They are planning on adding more full-text sources to the archives in the near future.

**Authority:** Pulitzer Prize Board

### The Tony Awards

http://www.tonys.org/

Articles, photos, interviews, current and past nominees and winners of the Tony award are available from this searchable archive. The site also lists current nominees' and other related feature articles.

**Authority:** Tony Award Productions

# Psychology

### Encyclopedia of Psychology

http://www.psychology.org/

"The Encyclopedia of Psychology is intended to facilitate browsing in any area of psychology." The database is restricted to links "providing information about scientific psychology." Each link is annotated and includes the add date. The site is keyword-searchable.  ∞

**Authority:** Psychology.org

### PsycSite: Science of Psychology Resources Site

http://stange.simplenet.com/psycsite/

Click on the brain to enter the site. "PsycSite is a non-profit, public-service Internet Site for psychologists, psychology students and anyone else interested in the science of psychology." The 5,000+ links are organized into a table with various categories such as Acknowledgments, Informational Resources, Student Centre, Professional Centre and Research Centre. There is a great page of "Helpful Hints" to help you use the page more effectively. There is currently no search engine on this site.  ∞

**Authority:** Ken Stange, Dept. of Psychology, Nipissing University

### Social Psychology Network

http://www.socialpsychology.org/

Available on the WWW since 1996, the Social Psychology Network claims to be "the largest social psychology database on the Internet. In these pages, you'll find more than 5,000 links to psychology-related resources." The site has arranged the links into categories such as General Psychology, Electronic Forums and Social Psychology. There is a keyword search option.  ∞

**Authority:** Professor Scott Plous, Dept. of Psychology, Wesleyan University

# Quotations (*see also* Full-Text Resources; History; Reading and Literature)

### Quotations

http://www.bartleby.com/quotations/

Project Bartleby has made available the full-text of Bartlett's 1901 edition *Familiar Quotations*, the 1996 *Columbia World of Quotations* and the 1988 Simpson's

*Contemporary Quotations*, providing access to hundreds if not thousands of quotes from reputable publishers. You can search all of the works either collectively or individually by keyword. Alternately you can click on the individual work and browse by author, title or subject.

**Authority:** Project Bartleby

## Quotations Page

http://www.quotationspage.com/

Be aware that this may not be the most authoritative of sites, but it does include a lot of quotations and links to other quotation sites. Quotes can be submitted by anyone and do not appear to be verified for accuracy.

**Authority:** Michael Moncur and Starling Technologies

## Quoteland.com

http://www.quoteland.com/

One of the most outstanding things about this site is the bibliography or resources used in compiling the quotes which include resources such as *Hoyt's New Cyclopedia of Practical Quotations* and *Treasury of Presidential Quotations*. The site is keyword-searchable or browsable by topic or author. A particularly useful feature is the "Identify a Quote" option that helps to find who actually said/wrote a particular phrase. Be sure to read the instructions thoroughly. ∞

**Authority:** David Borenstein and Adam Lewis, Quoteland.com

# <u>Reading and Literature</u> (*see also* Full-Text Resources; Grammar, Writing and Style Guides)

## AlphaBits for Kids

http://www.edu4kids.com/alpha/

This online game is useful for drilling alphabet recognition. The options for play include: find the letter that comes before, find the matching letter, find the missing letter and find the letter that comes after. (Grades PreK–1)

**Authority:** Infobahn Xpress and Tomas Rivera Elementry School, Riverside California

## Carol Hurst's Children's Literature Site

http://www.carolhurst.com/

An award-winning site that is "a collection of reviews of great books for kids, ideas of ways to use them in the classroom and collections of books and activities about particular subjects, curriculum areas, themes and professional topics." Examples, annotated and recommended links and books, articles, illustrations and other informa-

tion make this site one of the most useful children's literature sites on the Web. Much of the information comes from Carol Hurst's professional writings. ∞

**Authority:** Carol Otis Hurst and Rebecca Otis

## Children's Literature & Language Arts Resources

http://falcon.jmu.edu/~ramseyil/childlit.htm

"This page focuses on children's literature in education. Teachers, library media professionals, parents and students will find information on children's literature and associated language arts here." This site indexes other websites into the following areas: Book Awards, Book & Media Reviews, Authors & Illustrators, The Genres, Bibliotherapy, The "isms," Literary Enrichment Activities, Book Fairs & Literary Festivals, Want to Talk? Newsgroups, Chats... and Other Children's Literature Sites. ∞

**Authority:** Inez Ramsey, James Madison University

## Children's Literature Web Guide

http://www.acs.ucalgary.ca/~dkbrown/

This up-to-date site has several sections: Features, Discussion Boards, Quick Reference and More Links. Within these sections are discussion areas, annotated lists of links, lists of award-winning children's literature, a conference bulletin board, children's best sellers and resources for teachers, parents, storytellers, writers and illustrators. ∞

**Authority:** David K. Brown, Director, Doucette Library of Teaching Resources, University of Calgary

## Dr. Seuss' Seussville!

http://www.randomhouse.com/seussville/

A fun page created just for kids. There are activities designed around various Dr. Seuss books. Activities include art, games, recipes and reading. (Grades PreK–8)

**Authority:** Dr. Seuss Enterprises, L.P.

## Learning to Read

http://www.toread.com/

"The purpose of this Web page is to improve the quality of reading instruction through the study of the reading process and teaching techniques. It will serve as a clearinghouse for the dissemination of reading research through conferences, journals and other publications." The site also contains links to interactive lessons, publisher/author pages and recommended books. (Grades K–12) ✎

**Authority:** John Nemes

## Word Detective

http://www.word-detective.com/

This fun site is the "online version of The Word Detective, a newspaper column answering readers' questions about words and language." Scroll down the page to find back issues including hundreds of words and phrases indexed in alphabetical order. Also includes links to other language sites. (Grades 7–Undergraduate)

**Authority:** Evan Morris

## World of Reading

http://www.worldreading.org/

A great site of book reviews by kids, for kids. Children of all ages are encouraged to submit reviews on any kind of book they wish. All reviews are screened before being posted. The site "is designed to be an educational, challenging and safe website. Its purpose is to excite children about reading, writing and publishing." (Grades 2–7)

**Authority:** Mary P. Timmons, Director, World of Reading

# Recipes

## All Recipes

http://www.allrecipes.com/

All Recipes is a "community-based recipe and meal planning website." Recipes are submitted by individuals and include user ratings, complete instructions and cooking times. A great feature on the site is the ability print out the recipes in 3x5", 4x6" and full-page formats. If you've "joined" the site, you can automatically add the ingredients from the recipe to your Shopping List. Another useful feature is the ability to convert the recipe from metric to U.S. standard and back. There is a special section for kids recipes. The site is searchable and has a browsable index.

**Authority:** Allrecipes.com

## CopyKat Creations

http://www.copykat.com/

The recipes in this database are based on the menus of restaurants such as Red Lobster, Boston Market, Olive Garden and Marie Callendars. Find individual recipes by clicking on CopyKat Recipes and then search by keyword, select a category like breads or main dishes or select a letter in the alphabet. Since all recipes begin with the name of the restaurant of origin, the alphabetic list functions as a list of recipes from specific restaurants. There are other resources on this site, including links to other cooking websites and Generations, a family cookbook.

**Authority:** CopyKat Creations

## KidsKuisine

http://www.kidskuisine.com/

Created by the folks at CopyKat Creations, this is a companion site of "recipes for kids and recipes kids can make." It is divided into the following sections: Cooking with Kids, Fun to Make, Seasonal and Cooking for Kids. Within each section are the similar searching options as the parent CopyKat site, including keyword search and food category browse. Many of the recipes include color photos.

**Authority:** CopyKat Creations

## RecipeLand

http://www.recipeland.com/

This utilitarian site has more than 48,000 recipes and is still growing. The index is accessible in several ways including: Find by Category, Find by Title and Find by All. The site also contains many recipe reviews, a mailing list, FAQ and discussion forums.

**Authority:** metro.isp Inc.

## RecipeSource

http://www.recipesource.com/

This site began with the collection of hundreds of recipes from the mailing lists and newsgroups available in 1993. The site went online in 1995 as SOAR: The Searchable Online Archive of Recipes. Today it contains more than 70,000 recipes categorized by region and type. The search engine is capable of using pluses, minuses and quotation marks. There are plans for adding ingredient searching in the near future.

**Authority:** Jennifer Snider Coopersmith, Alan Coopersmith, Kenji Hubbard, Elaine Chao, RecipeSource

## Tasty Insect Recipes

http://www.ent.iastate.edu/misc/insectsasfood.html

This is probably the site with the most unusual recipes. They are listed on the left side bar along with Nutrition, More Treats and Where to Buy Insects. The site disclaimer reads: "The Department of Entomology at Iowa State University is not responsible for gastric distress, allergic reactions, feelings of repulsion or other problems resulting from the ingestion of foods represented on these pages."

**Authority:** Entomology Dept., Iowa State University

## Vegetarian Recipes Around the World

http://www.ivu.org/recipes/

Sponsored by the International Vegetarian Union, this page includes all kinds of recipes from places such as Africa, India, Pakistan, the Caribbean and Greece.

Standard western favorites are also included. Recipes can be found by browsing by region or by using search feature. Searches can be narrowed by various subjects (i.e., Holidays or East Asian) and formats (i.e., Long or Short).

**Authority:** John Davis, International Vegetarian Union

## Reference: Other Virtual Reference Sites

### Internet Public Library: Ready Reference Collection

http://www.ipl.org/ref/RR/

The authoritative site states that "sources are selected according to ease of use, quality and quantity of information, frequency of updating and authoritativeness." It is divided by subject category and includes a search engine at the bottom of the site. ∞

**Authority:** Internet Public Library

### Martindale's

http://www-sci.lib.uci.edu/HSG/Ref.html

While it seems a bit disorganized, this site has extensive links to reference resources arranged by subject. No overriding collection development goal is stated, but from the sheer number of sites listed it would seem that the idea is to collect the entirety of web reference sources. It has strong collections in the sciences. The RefDesk and MEL sites described below are a better sources for finding quick look-up reference tools, but, Martindale's makes a good third choice when hunting for resources. ∞

**Authority:** Jim Martindale

### MEL: Reference Desk

http://mel.lib.mi.us/reference/REF-index.html

The extensive list of sources on this site have been collected under the following guidelines: "reference tools which should be of immediate value to librarians responding to inquiries from public library clients. Thus works of interest primarily to scientists, academic researchers and technicians are not included. These resources provide short concise answers to queries, are normally arranged in a format that makes the information easily accessible and may cover any subject area." While the tools are collected for public librarians, a lot of the sites are relevant to school libraries and media centers. ∞

**Authority:** Michigan Electronic Library

### RefDesk.com

http://www.refdesk.com

RefDesk.com is probably the single largest collection of reference resources. The goal of this site seems to be to index every page on the Web that might be related to reference. The Site Map is particularly valuable considering the overwhelming number of links and choices on the first page. For more selective and evaluated sources use the Internet Public Library or MEL. ∞

**Authority:** Bob Drudge

### U.S. Government Documents: Ready Reference Collection

http://www.columbia.edu/cu/lweb/indiv/dsc/readyref.html

This official site collects U.S. government sources that can be used for reference inquiries. Some of the sources listed on the page are available in libraries only, but most have html or .pdf versions. The site is arranged by the following subjects: General, Agriculture, Business/Economics, Census & Demographics, Crime & Justice, Education, Energy, Environment, Foreign Countries, Government & Law, Health & Social Services, Military, Minerals & Mining, Science & Engineering and Transportation. This is an excellent source for statistical information. ∞

**Authority:** Columbia University Libraries

## Religion (*see also* Full-Text Resources; History; Social Studies)

### The Catholic Encyclopedia

http://www.newadvent.org/cathen/

Originally published in 1908, this encyclopedia has articles on a myriad of topics. The site is arranged in a rough A through Z format. At this time no search engine is available. Each article is several paragraphs in length. Some entries such as the list of popes, have been updated. Look for information about saints, people, places, activities, dates, celebrations and other topics related to Catholicism.

**Authority:** Kevin Knight, New Advent

### Internet Sacred Text Archive

http://www.sacred-texts.com/

"This site is intended to be a freely available archive of significant primary texts relating to religion and mythology. Texts are presented in English translation and, in some cases, in the original language." To begin, choose from one of the following: Eastern, Western, Traditional or Esoteric to access such diverse texts as the Bible, Koran and Confucian Canon.

**Authority:** J.B. Hare.

## Virtual Religion Index

http://religion.rutgers.edu/vri/

This enormous site has hundreds of annotated links arranged into the categories such as Ancient Near East, Ethics & Moral Values, Hindu Studies, Jewish Studies and Biblical Studies. No search engine is available, but that does not detract from the value of this site.

**Authority:** Dept. of Religion, Rutgers University

# Science (*see also* Chemistry; Mathematics; Physics and Astronomy)

## Explorer

http://explorer.scrtec.org/explorer/

Explorer is a "collection of educational resources (instructional software, lab activities, lesson plans, student created materials ...) for K–12 mathematics and science education." It is searchable by description, author or title. You can also browse through the lesson plans by clicking on either the Mathematics Curriculum or the Natural Science Curriculum buttons. (Grades K–12)

**Authority:** Great Lakes Collaborative and UNITE Group, University of Kansas

## Frank Potter's Science Gems

http://www.sciencegems.com/

Frank Potter has created a wonderful index to science resources on the Web for grades K–16. The index includes more than "14,000 Science Resources sorted by Category, Subcategory and Grade Level." It is searchable by keyword. (Grades K–16)

**Authority:** Frank Potter

## GreatScopes

http://www.greatscopes.com/activity.htm

The site subtitle reads: "Activities and experiments for microscopists young and old." The activities include Finding Bacteria in Yogurt, Examining in Pond Weed Cells and Fiber Detective! Click on "Glossary" to view a picture of a microscope with all the parts labeled and named, to read the microscope buying guide and to get definitions for microscope-related words. (Grades 6–12)

**Authority:** John E. Lind

## How Stuff Works

http://www.howstuffworks.com/

This astonishing site has articles on how everything imaginable works. Each article includes illustrations, references and web links. The site is arranged into the following categories such as: Computers & Internet,

Engines & Automotive, Electronics & Telecom and Science & Technology. (Grades 6–12)

**Authority:** Howstuffworks, Inc.

## Learning Studio at the Exploratorium

http://www.exploratorium.edu/learning_studio/index.html

The Exploratorium has created various online experimental multimedia learning exhibits, such as a cow's eye dissection. The Science Snackbook Series offers "miniature science exhibits that teachers can make using common, inexpensive, easily available materials." (Grades 3–9)

**Authority:** Exploratorium

## Newton's Apple: Teacher's Guides

http://www.pbs.org/ktca/newtons/alpha.html

This is a companion site to the popular PBS show Newton's Apple. The teacher guides are arranged in alphabetical order by topic. It is not necessary to view or use the show in order to use the guides. Each science topic includes discussion information, vocabulary words, other resource lists and activities/experiments. Topics covered by Newton's Apple and this site include diabetes, black holes, compact discs, spelunking, drinking water and bicycles. (Grades 7–12)

**Authority:** Newton's Apple

## Project Primary

http://www.owu.edu/~mggrote/pp/

This amazing site is a "collaboration of professors from the departments of Botany-Microbiology, Chemistry, Education, Geology, Physics and Zoology at Ohio Wesleyan University and K–3 teachers from Ohio's Delaware, Marion and Union Counties to produce hands-on activities for the teaching of science." Lesson plans can be found for botany, chemistry, children's literature, geology, physics and zoology. (Grades K–3)

**Authority:** Project Primary

## Science Learning Network

http://www.sln.org/

Museums, educators, students and schools come together to provide science learning resources via the Internet. From the front page you can explore three main areas. 1. Check Out News and Links accesses lists of hotlinks from the museums associated with the network. 2. Visit our Museums goes to a list of participating museums. 3. Explore Our Resources gets to the centerpiece of site, where links to and descriptions of activities and resources on various scientific topics reside. (Grades 6–12)

**Authority:** Science Learning Network

### Virtual Field Trip

http://www.field-guides.com/

This cool site "is devoted to providing on-line field trips that take you to places that until now you could only dream about and teach you things you might not otherwise learn." Each field trip covers a single topic and contains resources and guides for teachers to use in conjunction with the trip. Some of the available trips include: Deserts, Fierce Creatures, Hurricanes, Sharks, Tornadoes and Volcanoes. (Grades K–8)

**Authority:** Tramline, Inc.

## Science Fairs

### Bunsen Bob's Science Hunt

http://www.sciencehunt.com/

Bunsen Bob's appealing website has indexed many other science fair websites, written articles explaining the various parts of a science project and created a wonderful resource to begin working on a science fair project. The resources are arranged under the following categories: Project Central, Science on Display, How Judges Think, Science Hunting, Finding Materials, Mom & Dad Zone and Talk Back. The site is keyword-searchable.

**Authority:** Hunt Corporation

### Science Fair Project Resource Guide

http://www.ipl.org/youth/projectguide/

Sponsored by the Internet Public Library, this site begins with introductory material about science fairs, the scientific method, choosing a topic and resources. There are embedded links in this section that refer to more text and lists of related links. Further down the page is an annotated list of websites that provide step-by-step instructions for science fair projects of all kinds.

**Authority:** Internet Public Library

### ScienzFair Projects

http://members.aol.com/ScienzFair/ideas.htm

Hundreds of science fair ideas are located on this site. "Most are not fully developed projects, but just ideas and outlines. It is left to the student to fully develop the project." The contents are arranged in subject category such as Anthropology & Sociology, Botany and Competitive Projects. The site is searchable but you must scroll to the bottom of the page to find the link to the search engine.

**Authority:** Sean McCormick of Weblink Consultants

## Search Engines: Directory

**Note:** Directory search engines are arranged by subject category. They are compiled by humans, not by computer programs, and they are frequently partnered with one or more standard search engines.

### LookSmart

http://www.looksmart.com/

LookSmart was founded in 1996. It has more than 200,000 categories. Secondary results come from the Inktomi database.

**Authority:** LookSmart

### Open Directory

http://www.dmoz.org

Open Directory is unique in that it has distributed the responsibility of creating the directory to subject volunteers throughout the world. It has more than 361,000 categories.

**Authority:** Open Directory

### Yahoo!

http://www.yahoo.com

Probably the oldest search engine on the Internet, Yahoo! began as a simple subject directory and evolved over time. It can search for phrases, titles and URLs. You can also use truncation, AND and OR. Secondary results come from Google.

**Authority:** Yahoo! Inc.

## Search Engines: For Kids

### Ask Jeeves For Kids

http://www.ajkids.com/

Like the standard AskJeeves, you can search the extensive database by typing a question into the search box. The meta search engine results come from Yahooligans, Education World and Federal Education Resources.

**Authority:** AskJeeves

### Awesome Library

http://www.awesomelibrary.org/

The "Awesome Library organizes the Web with 17,000 carefully reviewed resources, including the top 5 percent in education." Use the search box to find lesson plans, worksheets and websites on your topic. Alternately, you can browse through the subject categories such as English, Lessons, Reference and Social Studies.

**Authority:** EDI and Dr. R. Jerry Adams

### KidsClick!

http://sunsite.berkeley.edu/KidsClick!/

"KidsClick! was created by a group of librarians at the Ramapo Catskill Library System, as a logical step in addressing concerns about the role of public libraries in guiding their young users to valuable and age-appropriate websites." Every site in the index is annotated with notes for illustrations, reading level and subject. The site is keyword-searchable or browsable using the 600+ subject areas.

**Authority:** Ramapo Catskill Library System and Colorado State Library

### TekMom's

http://www.tekmom.com/search/

This site was designed to "provide research options for students who need to do Web searches, but who might not want to use the popular search engines which return links from the entire Web." Search engines included on this site are more than a dozen great search sites including: Yahooligans, Education World, SeaWorld Animal Info. Database, American Memories, Amazing Picture Machine and Encyclopedia.com.

**Authority:** Anne Savage

### Yahooligans!

http://www.yahooligans.com/

Produced by Yahoo! this goes beyond indexing websites by providing a Teachers' Guide with suggestions for teaching Internet Literacy and sample lesson plans. The search engine can be browsed by subject category or searched by keyword.

**Authority:** Yahooligans!

# Search Engines: Meta or Multiple

### Ask Jeeves

http://www.askjeeves.com

Query this user-friendly search engine by typing a question in the search box. After the search is run, several clarifying options will appear, click on "Ask" to go to any of those options. Even farther down the page the search will be executed on and retrieve results from other search engines. The resulting web pages appear in the Ask Jeeves frame, but the frame can be "clicked off" at any time. I use this search engine if I am not having any luck in finding the right search terms.

**Authority:** Ask Jeeves, Inc.

### Dogpile

http://www.dogpile.com/

Dogpile is my favorite meta search engine. This terrific search tool searches many different search engines, directories and specialty search sites. Doing a web search will result in a list of sites found by each engine with some sites being listed by one or more search engines.

**Authority:** Dogpile

### Mamma

http://www.mamma.com

Billed as "The Mother of All Search Engines," this site has been on the Web since 1996. Like MetaCrawler, the results are listed by relevance and the names of the contributing search engines are listed below each site. Mamma also searches for MP3s, images, news, audio and video files.

**Authority:** Mamma.com

### MetaCrawler

http://www.metacrawler.com/

Probably the oldest of the meta search engines, it was founded in 1995. It returns results based on relevancy ranking. The name(s) of the search engines that found the entry are listed. Entries that are found in multiple search engines are listed higher than results found by only one search engine.

**Authority:** MetaCrawler

### SurfWax

http://www.surfwax.com/

While SurfWax is a relative newcomer to the meta search engine world, it provides some of the best results. It displays the title of the retrieved site and the name of the contributing database. Duplicate listings are removed and results can be sorted by source, relevancy or in alphabetical order.

**Authority:** SurfWax Inc.

# Search Engines: Specialized

### Bomis.com

http://www.bomis.com

Web rings are intricate links shared by a group of sites based on a specific subject. There are thousands of web rings and they cover topics that range from a specific celebrity to dentistry. Bomis both sponsors web rings and indexes them. Browsing through a web ring is a great way to find related sites.

**Authority:** Bomis.com

## Ditto

http://www.ditto.com/

This search engine's index is created solely of images from web pages on the net. Just because an image is in this database does not mean it is copyright free. Search results are displayed in a thumbnail format with links to the site of origin.

**Authority:** Ditto.com

## Internets

http://www.internets.com

This unique search engine actually searches for subject-specific search engines. Type a subject discipline, concept or broad topic such as physics in the Find an Engine box, and you'll get a list of subject specific databases. Alternately use the pop-up Categories list.

**Authority:** wwwINTERNETS, Inc.

## RingSurf

http://www.ringsurf.com/

RingSurf is another search engine and host for web rings. Since each of the web ring search engines are also hosts, the indexes consist of the hosted web rings. This means you might need to try more than one of this type of search engine to find a relevant web ring.

**Authority:** RingSurf

## Search Engine Colossus

http://www.searchenginecolossus.com

Search engines of all kinds are organized first by country of origin and then alphabetically on this enormous site. Use this site to find country, and in some cases, city or state-specific search engines. Recently, subject categories have been added to the main list.

**Authority:** Bryan Strome

## SpeechBot

http://speechbot.research.compaq.com/

"SpeechBot is a search engine for audio & video content that is hosted and played from other websites." Currently there are only 20+ sites, mostly from popular radio programs, being indexed and transcribed. "Transcripts of the content based on speech recognition are not exact."

**Authority:** Compaq Corporate Research

## Yahoo! WebRing

http://dir.webring.yahoo.com/rw

Yahoo! now sponsors web rings and indexes them on this site.

**Authority:** Yahoo!

# Search Engines: Standard

**Note:** All of these search engines have the following things in common: help information, phrase searching using quotation marks, use of the plus sign, meaning "required word," use of the minus sign, meaning "excluded word" and advanced search features. Many of these search engines allow for Boolean logic searching the use of AND or and NOT.

## AltaVista

http://www.altavista.com/

One of my favorite search engines, it is case-sensitive and includes some of the most advanced search capabilities around. You can search by domain, applet, host, image, text, title and URL. The index for this search engine ranks consistently within the top tier as far as number of addresses in the database. Currently, it is associated with the LookSmart Directory for listings arranged by subject.

**Authority:** AltaVista

## Excite

http://www.excite.com

Excite uses a unique algorithm which matches not just the words entered into the search box, but words that are closely related. Unfortunately, if you do not use the plus signs in front of the entered words, it will do the search as if the words had an "or" between them. Excite has partnered with LookSmart for the listings arranged by subject. Excite owns both the Magellan and WebCrawler search engines.

**Authority:** Excite

## Fast Search

http://www.alltheweb.com

Also known as "alltheweb," this search engine purports to be the fastest at retrieving results. Along with the fully featured keyword search, you can search for pictures, videos, MP3 files and FTP files. The index for the search engine consistently ranks in the top tier for size of database.

**Authority:** Fast

## Google

http://www.google.com

If I had to choose just one search engine to use it would be Google. It consistently retrieves relevant results and is in the top tier for size of database. Use the advanced search features to search by domain, language or Boolean operators. Google provides some results for Yahoo and Netscape Search. Currently, the subject directory is associated with Open Directory.

**Authority:** Google

## HotBot

http://www.hotbot.com

Hotbot is owned and managed by Lycos. I am including it here because it has easy-to-use advanced searching capability. You can limit your search to sites with pictures, sound files, video or javascript by just checking one of the boxes on the left.

**Authority:** Lycos

## Lycos

http://www.lycos.com

Unfortunately, Lycos no longer creates a web database of its own. Its primary results come from the Open Directory and the secondary ones from the FAST search engine. However, it can be very useful when you are looking for information that a hobbyist or fan would provide on a web page such as recipes, crafts or model trains. Lycos is the owner of both Tripod and Angelfire, free web page hosting services, thereby making searchable hundreds perhaps even thousands of individual, personal web pages.

**Authority:** Lycos

## Northern Light

http://www.northernlight.com

This is another search engine I recommend. Northern Light combines a standard search engine with its own special collection database. The special collection access over 7,100 journals, reviews, books, magazines and news wires. Information from the special collection is not free, but is purchased one article at a time. Prices range from $1.00 to $4.00 with a few "higher value sources, such as Investext reports costing more."

**Authority:** Northern Lights

# Social Studies (*see also* History; International Country Information; Philosophy)

## Anthropology Internet Resources

http://www.wcsu.ctstateu.edu/socialsci/antres.html

This simple index of anthropology-related websites is searchable by keyword or browsable by category. There are more than 100 websites divided into the following categories: Culture, Linguistics, Physical Anthropology, Archaeology, Native American, General Sources and Miscellaneous. ∞

**Authority:** Dept. of Social Studies, Western Connecticut State University

## Cultural Arts Resources for Teachers and Students

http://www.carts.org/

C.A.R.T.S. is a project "whose mission is to document, preserve and present the living cultural heritage of New York and other cities." Under the "Resources" heading is a geographically arranged set of links to arts councils, heritage projects, museums, folk arts and other websites celebrating or providing cultural information. ∞

**Authority:** City Lore

## Native American Sites

http://www.nativeculture.com/lisamitten/indians.html

The goal of this site is to "provide access to home pages of individual Native Americans and Nations and to other sites that provide solid information about American Indians." The site is divided many sections such as Individual Native Nations, Native Organizations, Languages, The Mascot Issue and Native Authors. Each site on these lists includes a brief annotation and the date when it was added to the index. ∞

**Authority:** Lisa Mitten, Social Sciences Subject Editor, CHOICE Magazine

## NativeTech

http://www.nativetech.org/

NativeTech is a creative site which includes original articles, charts, illustrations, activities and lessons about Native American technology and art. The entries are divided into the following categories: Beadwork, Birds & Feathers, Clay & Pottery, Games & Toys, Leather & Clothes, Metalwork, Plants & Trees, Porcupine Quills, Stonework & Tools, Weaving & Cordage, Essays & Articles, Food & Recipes, Poetry & Stories, Contemporary Issues and Instructional Pamphlets.

**Authority:** Tara Prindle

## Say Hello to the World

http://www.ipl.org/youth/hello/

Sponsored by the Internet Public Library, the "goal of this project is to bring together language resources on the Internet into one convenient place for beginners who would like to learn more about languages from all over the world." There are sound files for "hello" in more than 29 different languages. The site includes a list of languages and language resources under the "And many more" link. ∞

**Authority:** Lorri Mon and the Internet Public Library

### Social, Economic and Political Change

http://gsociology.icaap.org/

The principle aim of this site is to "present information that can be used to explain historical change, growth and development." The links and resources are arranged under the following annotated subject categories: Summary, Theory, Data, National Profiles, History, Research organizations, Links, Bibliographies and syllabi, Other and Software.

**Authority:** Gene Shackman, School of Public Health, SUNY Albany

### Social Studies Lesson Plans and Resources

http://www.csun.edu/~hcedu013/index.html

This easy-to-use site is arranged into categories such as Lesson Plans and Teaching Strategies, Online Activities and What's New This Month. Lesson plans are marked with appropriate grade level designations and range from Art and Life in Africa Project to Judges in the Classroom. (Grades K–12) ∞

**Authority:** Dr. Marty Levine, Professor of Secondary Education, California State University, Northridge

### Social Studies Sources

http://education.indiana.edu/~socialst/

"This page is designed primarily for K–12 social studies teachers and students. It also has information and topics that are useful to preservice social studies instructors and students." Websites are organized under the following subject areas: Diversity, General History, Geography, Government, News Sources, U.S. History and World History.

**Authority:** Fred Risinger, Director of Professional Development, School Services and Summer Sessions, School of Education, Indiana University, Bloomington.

### World Ethnic Survey

http://www.partal.com/ciemen/ethnic.html

"Search for information on ethnic, native and nationalists affairs all over the world" on this site. It is arranged by geographic region and then in alphabetical order by title. There are sites on geographic regions such as Corsica, Tibet, East Timor and Sudan. ∞

**Authority:** CIEMEN, Centre Internacional Escarre per a les Minories Etniques i Nacionals

# Sports

### ESPN.com

http://espn.go.com/main.html

This is the official ESPN site. It includes scores, programming schedules, statistics, news and more. It is searchable by keyword or browsable via the sport topics on the left button bar.

**Authority:** ESPN

### HickokSports.com—History

http://www.hickoksports.com/history.shtml

Ralph Hickok, well-known author of books such as "The Encyclopedia of North American Sports History" has created this site about the history of sports. The extensive articles are arranged into several browsable lists including Alpha Index, Index by Sport and History Bits. The articles include such diverse topics as Boxing, Bocce, Fencing and the Kentucky Derby. Other sections on the site include Ask a Question, Visit the Forum, Archives and General Links. The site is searchable.

**Authority:** Ralph Hickok

### Sports Network

http://www.sportsnetwork.com/home.asp

"The Sports Network provides up-to-the-second sports scores, statistics, news, injury and weather reports, standings, schedules, team information and a lot more." It includes all kinds of sports but the main focus is on popular ones such as Baseball, Football, Soccer, Auto Racing and Cricket.

**Authority:** Sports Network

### Sports Resources

http://www.ipl.org/ref/RR/static/ent80.00.00.html

The Internet Public Library has created this fabulous directory to sports resources on the Internet. It is arranged by sport at the top of the page. As you scroll to the bottom you access many general sports resources. All links are annotated and include authors, subjects and keywords. ∞

**Authority:** Internet Public Library

# Statistics (*see also* Mathematics)

**Note:** Statistics can be found in many places. The sites listed here are some of the best and most comprehensive. Try more than one of these to make certain you have done a thorough search. The most extensive site is "Statistical Resources on the Web," provided by the University of Michigan.

## Census Bureau Home Page

http://www.census.gov/

The United States Census Bureau provides internet access to a staggering array of statistical information. Housing, population and income figures are representative of the kinds of statistics to be found on this site. The site can be browsed by subject or searched by keyword. Click on "Related Sites" to access other statistical federal, state and international statistics sites.

**Authority:** U.S. Census Bureau

## County and City Databooks

http://fisher.lib.Virginia.EDU/ccdb/

This useful site includes the full-text of the 1988 and 1994 County and City Databooks. Search this database of state and county level census data by keyword. Includes information on persons per square mile, housing by structure type, serious crimes and much more. Results of searches can be viewed as pages or tables and can be downloaded.

**Authority:** Geospatial and Statistical Data Center

## Encyclopedia of Education Stats

http://nces.ed.gov/edstats/

Statistics on everything related to education can be found on this Web page. It is keyword-searchable or browsable via subject. The Encyclopedia includes the full-text of the following: The Condition of Education, The Digest of Education Statistics, Education Indicators: an International Perspective and Youth Indicators.

**Authority:** U.S. National Center for Education Statistics (NCES)

## Geospatial and Statistical Data Center

http://fisher.lib.virginia.edu/

This Web page provides comprehensive access to "extensive collections of numeric and geospatial data files, computing facilities and software for data manipulation, research and instruction and a suite of Internet-accessible data extraction tools." Click on "Interactive Data" to get to the National and International statistical databases. There are four main categories of information: Domestic Economic Data, Educational Data, Historical Data and International Economic Data. Because this site is created and hosted by the University of Virginia library, many items are for the state of Virginia or are located in this particular library.

**Authority:** Geospatial and Statistical Data Center

## Government Information Sharing Project

http://govinfo.library.orst.edu/

A wide range of online government documents are arranged first by subject category and then by geographic region. The site includes lots of "help" information.

**Authority:** U.S. Government and the Government Information Sharing Project

## Infonation

http://www.un.org/Pubs/CyberSchoolBus/infonation/e_infonation.htm

Solid, factual statistics are found in this database of comparative information for countries that are members of the United Nations. You can select up to seven countries and then choose from four broad categories: Geography, Economy, Population and Social Indicators to create comparative data sets. Tables and lists of comparative variables include literacy rates, population, unemployment and highest average temperature, among others.

**Authority:** United Nations

## International Data Base

http://www.census.gov/ipc/www/idbnew.html

This official site has demographic and socio-economic statistical data for 227 countries and areas of the world. Historical coverage dates back to 1950. It also projects demographic data forward to 2050.

**Authority:** U.S. Bureau of the Census

## Statistical Resources on the Web

http://www.lib.umich.edu/libhome/Documents.center/stats.html

This is the best place to start looking for statistical information. Hundreds of statistical sources are indexed and annotated on this site. Use the search engine, alphabetical link directory or browse through the subject categories to find entries. ∞

**Authority:** Documents Center, University of Michigan

## Uniform Crime Reports

http://fisher.lib.virginia.edu/crime/

The Uniform Crime Reports provides county-level crime statistics for 1990–1998. This site includes statistical information about crimes rates for assault, burglary, larceny, fraud, murder, embezzlement, vandalism, vagrancy, forgery and more. Results of searches can be viewed as pages or tables and can be downloaded.

**Authority:** Geospatial and Statical Data Center

# Symbols (*see also* Arts)

## SYMBOLS.com: Encyclopedia of Western Signs and Ideograms

http://www.SYMBOLS.com/

An interesting site with definitions for many commonly used symbols. The database is searchable via symbol graphic or browsable by word. The site contains over 2,500 signs "arranged into 54 groups according to their graphic characteristics. In 1,600 articles their histories, uses and meanings are thoroughly discussed. The signs range from ideograms carved in mammoth teeth by Cro-Magnon men, to hobo signs and subway graffiti." There are extensive help screens available.

**Authority:** Carl G. Liungman

# Thesauri (*see also* Dictionaries; Reference: Other Virtual Reference Sites)

## Bartleby.com: Thesauri

http://www.bartleby.com/thesauri/

Project Bartleby has provided the full-text to *Roget's II: The New Thesaurus* (3rd edition 1995) and *Roget's International Thesaurus of English Words and Phrases* (1922). Both books can be searched simultaneously or individually by keyword. Alternately you can click on the title for either book and browse through the alphabetical index. Hyperlinked cross-references are used extensively.

**Authority:** Peter Roget, C. O. Sylvester Mawson, American Heritage Dictionaries and Bartleby.com

## Thesaurus.com

http://www.thesaurus.com/

Thesaurus.com uses linking to great effect. It allows you to browse through the thesaurus by clicking through various word meanings. For instance, "walk" retrieves 27 different definition concepts such as journey, amusement, conduct and life. Each concept includes words and phrases that can replace the word "walk" in a sentence. Thesaurus.com is twinned to the Dictionary.com site, making the searching for word meanings, synonyms and usage seamless.

**Authority:** Lexico LLC.

## Web Thesaurus Compendium

http://www-cui.darmstadt.gmd.de/~lutes/thesauri.html

This is an amazing collection of both subject-specific and general thesauri. Access the information via an alphabetical title list or by a subject list.

**Authority:** Barbara Lutes

# Time (*see also* Calendars; Measurements)

## Horology

http://www.horology.com/horology/

"This page and subsidiary web pages attempt to provide a comprehensive Index and Crosslinks to as much Horological Information on the WWW as possible." The contents are arranged into broad categories such as The Exact Time Is, Horological Organizations and Timepieces. The site is searchable. Unfortunately, the site does not appear to be actively maintained. I am including it because there is a chance they will update it, links going to major organizations and sites still work and there is no other site like it on the Web.

**Authority:** Fortunat F. Mueller-Maerki

## Local Times Around the World

http://www.hilink.com.au/times/

"This guide attempts to list all of the world's countries and many of its islands, with a pointer to the local time in the region." The site is arranged by geographic region. Use this page by clicking on any of the continents. Entries include location, latitude, longitude, Greenwich Mean Time, Universal Coordinated Time, local time zone and daylight savings time information.

**Authority:** ClariNET Internet Solutions

## NIST Time and Frequency Historical Exhibits

http://www.bldrdoc.gov/timefreq/general/exhibits.html

The National Institute of Standards and Technology sponsors this informative site. It consists of five exhibits detailing in images, essays, links and references the history of time, calendars and timekeeping. The exhibits are titled: A Walk Through Time, Calendars Through the Ages, The Quartz Watch, Daylight Savings Time and NIST's Work Measuring Time & Frequency. NIST is responsible for the contents of the sections on the history of time and NIST's history. The other sections are from other sites on the Web.

**Authority:** U.S. National Institute of Standards and Technology

# Travel (*see also* International Country Information)

## CDC Travelers' Health

http://www.cdc.gov/travel/

The CDC provides this unique site which is not about choosing a good restaurant or hotel. This site is about staying healthy when you travel. And it isn't just for international travel. Information about disease outbreaks are available for the United States as well. The site provides reference materials and notices, and it makes health recommendations. You can begin using this site by either selecting a travel region or by browsing through the articles arranged within subjects such as vaccinations, outbreaks and traveling with children.

**Authority:** Center for Disease Control

## citysearch.com

http://www.citysearch.com/

There are two sections to this site, the first is for cities within the United States and the second is for international cities. You can search for your town by entering your zip code in the search box. Entries include events by calendar date, type, movies, local events, restaurants & bars, hotels & visitors.

**Authority:** Ticketmaster

## Excite Travel

http://travel.excite.com

Travel sites can be a little overwhelming at first, because they include a lot of advertising and sales information on products such as airline tickets, rental cars, cruises and hotel reservations. Look for a keyword search box to type in the name of your destination city and click send. The search results will bring back information about the city. This information is based upon what exists on the Web, so some cities have an overwhelming array of links and other locations have only a few. Travel sites usually provide information such as what to do, entertainment, education, theater schedules, restaurant reviews, hotel reviews, city facts, where to rent a car, travel tips and reservations. ∞

**Authority:** Excite

## Fodor's

http://www.fodors.com/

Fodor's is an unusual travel site in that it isn't indexing Internet information, but is providing reviews and information from their own travel guidebooks. They have articles on almost everything including: electricity, pets, packing and air travel. While they only include selected destinations, these destinations include cities both in the United States and around the world. The site includes restaurant, hotel, entertainment and travel tips for the cities it lists.

**Authority:** Fodor's

## Travel for Kids

http://www.travelforkids.com/

This site is a "family travel guide for planning vacation trips with children as fun adventures. Get tips on kid-

friendly 'must-see's,' discover hidden treasures and learn insider secrets for holidays in Europe, South America, Asia and now, North America." Currently there are only 28 countries listed on the site as destinations. The Travel Essentials category lists articles as diverse as "Traveling with Stuffed Animals" and "Safety Issues—Country Politics and Natural Disasters."

**Authority:** Globetracks, Inc.

## Travelocity

http://www.travelocity.com

You can make reservations for hotels, airlines, vacations, cruises and rental cars on this site. The best part of this site is the destination guide which provides country-level information including a brief overview of the destination, facts, when to go, activities and maps.

**Authority:** Travelocity

## USA CityLink

http://www.usacitylink.com/

This site is yet another travel site where you can book reservations for hotels and other services. Because this site concentrates on cities in the United States, it has more city and state guides and information. The site is based on what is available on the Web, therefore the contents will grow as the Internet does. CityLink has made agreements with several yellow page services to bring content when none has been indexed from the Web. ∞

**Authority:** USA CityLink

# United States: Federal Government

## Abbreviations and Acronyms of the U.S. Government

http://www.ulib.iupui.edu/subjectareas/gov/docs_abbrev.html

This single-page site is a fairly comprehensive list of U.S. Government abbreviations and acronyms. Each acronym is written out and includes a link to the "official" home page for the agency or program listed. For instance ABMC is the American Battle Monuments Commission and the link takes you to: http://www.abmc.gov/ the ABMC's main site.

**Authority:** Kelly Smith, University Library, Indiana University-Purdue University, Indianapolis

## Ben's Guide to U.S. Government for Kids

http://bensguide.gpo.gov/

A wonderful guide to the U.S. Government, Ben's guide is "a service of the Superintendent of

Documents, U.S. Government Printing Office (GPO)." It is designed to teach students how the U.S. government works and how to use GPO documents. The site includes lessons, articles, games and a special guide for teachers and parents. (Grades K–12)

**Authority:** U.S. Government Printing Office

### Contacting the Congress

http://www.visi.com/juan/congress/

Try this site for contact information for every United States Congress member. Click on the map or type in your zip code to get a geographical region's congressional membership information. You can fill in a congress member's name to get an individual's phone number, fax number, district phone number and e-mail address. Where possible, links to congress member's home pages are included.

**Authority:** Juan Cabanela

### THOMAS: U.S. Congress on the Internet

http://thomas.loc.gov/

This U.S. federal site accesses information relating to Congress and is divided into three sections: Legislation, Congressional Record and Committee Information. Bills, legislation, votes, roll calls, committee reports, directories, processes and historical documents are all here. Search the site by bill number or by keyword.

**Authority:** U.S. Congress

### The United States Government Manual

http://www.access.gpo.gov/nara/nara001.html

This site includes copies of the Manuals from 1995 to the present. The preface of this full-text book states that as "the official handbook of the Federal Government, *The United States Government Manual* provides comprehensive information on the agencies of the legislative, judicial and executive branches. The Manual also includes information on quasi-official agencies; international organizations in which the United States participates; and boards, commissions and committees." One or more of the manuals can be searched by keyword and the full text of each manual are available in both text and .pdf forms.

**Authority:** U.S. Government

### Virtual Tour of the U.S. Government

http://www.virtualfreesites.com/us-gov.html

A novel way to introduce the various branches of government to students. Tours are available for the White House, the Old Executive Office Building, the First Lady's Sculpture Garden, The Capitol, The Legislature, The Judiciary and more. This site is not creating the content, but is indexing other government related websites and information. ⚭

**Authority:** Virtual Sites

### The White House

http://www.whitehouse.gov/

Use the blue bar on the left of the page to navigate through the seven main site sections including: President, News, History, For Kids, Tours, Your Government and Appointments. Within these sections you can find articles, photos and other information relating to the presidency, presidents past and future, the White House and the U.S. government.

**Authority:** The White House

# United States: Search Engines

**Note:** Each U.S. government search engine indexes government sites in a different way. There is a lot of redundancy, but the indexes are not duplicating each other. When looking for government information be sure to try more than one search engine.

### FirstGov

http://www.firstgov.gov/

FirstGov is "the only official U.S. Government portal to 30 million pages of government information, services and online transactions." It is purported to index the entirety of every U.S. document. Many state and local government websites are included in the database. The index can be accessed via a search engine or through a topical directory.

**Authority:** U.S., Office of FirstGov, General Services Administration

### Google: UncleSam

http://www.google.com/unclesam

Google, my favorite search engine, has created Uncle Sam in order to facilitate the retrieval of U.S. government information. It may not be as comprehensive as FirstGov.

**Authority:** Google

### Government Information Locator Service (GILS)

http://www.access.gpo.gov/su_docs/gils/

"GILS records identify public information resources within the Federal Government, describe the information available in these resources and assist in obtaining the information." Which means that using this database will find information produced by the federal government. However, the database does not include all government agencies or their pages. The database is keyword-searchable and will allow AND or, NOT, ADJ, phrase and truncation searching.

**Authority:** U.S., Government Printing Office

### Government Sites for Kids

http://www.westga.edu/~library/depts/govdoc/kids.shtml

A nicely designed site that is browsable by subject or government agency. It includes only sites produced by the government that are created for kids. Included are subjects such as Aeronautics, Crime & Law Enforcement, Health and Money. (Grades K–12)

**Authority:** Michael Aldrich, Ingram Library, State University of West Georgia

### University of Michigan Documents Center

http://www.lib.umich.edu/govdocs/frames/fedfr.html

The University of Michigan created this comprehensive directory to U.S. government information. A detailed alphabetical list of subjects is located on the left. Larger subject categories such as Copyright and Historic Documents are arranged in the center of the main page. The site is searchable and includes a site map. The site map is an alphabetically arranged subject index.

**Authority:** Grace York, Coordinator, Documents Center, Library, University of Michigan

# United States: State Information (*see also* Atlases and Maps; Travel)

### 50 States and Capitals

http://www.50states.com/

If you are wondering what North Dakota's state song might be, you will find it here. Arranged in alphabetical order by state abbreviation, this site provides factual information for the 50 states and the commonwealths and territories of the United States. Note: This site occasionally does not underline its links, so everything you see in blue is clickable. (Grades 4–12)

**Authority:** Weber Communications

### Geobop's North America

http://www.geobop.com/World/NA/

This site is arranged alphabetically by U.S. state or Canadian province name. The list has links to information about the official symbols of the states and provinces. (Grades 4–12)

**Authority:** Geobopological Survey

### National Atlas of the United States of America

http://www-atlas.usgs.gov/

The United States Geological Survey (USGS) provides the maps for this clever site. Click on "Atlas Maps" to access the heart of this site. From here you can explore the many options available under "National Atlas Online, Interactive Map Browser." The first screen consists of detailed information on how to use the map browser. Click on "Go straight to the Map Browser" to continue. From here you select layers such as county boundaries, volcanoes, water features, railroads or airports and then click "Redraw" to show the features.

**Authority:** U.S. Department of the Interior

### Stately Knowledge

http://www.ipl.org/youth/stateknow

Arranged alphabetically by state, this site has basic factual information on all 50 states and Washington, D.C. Comparison charts for size and population, dates each state entered the union, charts of capitals, state birds and state flowers are available toward the bottom of the page. There are links to other resources about the state including encyclopedia articles and official state websites.

**Authority:** Stately Knowledge and the Internet Public Library

# Universities and Colleges

### American Universities

http://www.clas.ufl.edu/CLAS/american-universities.html

This comprehensive site lists the home pages for American universities granting bachelors or advanced degrees. It is arranged in alphabetical order by the name of the institution. In the first paragraphs introducing the site are links to three other websites, Community Colleges, Canadian Universities and International Universities. ∞

**Authority:** Mike Conlon, University of Florida

### College and University Rankings

http://www.library.uiuc.edu/edx/rankings.htm

This site is an eclectic list of websites that rank colleges and universities based such diverse topics as "most wired" and "character building." Kiplingers Top 100 and U.S. News and World Report College Rankings are probably some of the best-known ranking reports on this site. ∞

**Authority:** Education and Social Studies Library, University of Illinois, Urbana-Champaign

### College is Possible

http://www.collegeispossible.org/

Sponsored by the Coalition of America's Colleges and Universities, this site is a useful guide for parents and students. It is divided into three sections: Preparing for College, Choosing the Right College and Paying for College. Within the sections are articles such as "Avoiding Scholarship Scams" and "Responsible Borrowing." Articles frequently include a list of related links.

**Authority:** Coalition of America's Colleges and Universities

### FinAid!

http://www.finaid.org/

A not-for-profit site which can help anyone with their college financial planning. Articles with linking pages discuss at length topics like loans, student loans, Stafford loans, Perkins loans, parent loans, private loans and loan consolidation. Other major categories for information include: Scholarships, Other Types of Aid, Financial Aid Applications, Answering Your Questions, Calculators and Beyond Financial Aid.

**Authority:** Mark Kantrowitz

### Peterson's

http://www.petersons.com/

Peterson's Guides to colleges and universities are staple resources for most reference book collections. This commercial site has answers to all kinds of questions about going to college. Articles, links and information are organized into many subject categories such as "Chat online with a college counselor," "Study Abroad," and "Adult/Distance Learning Programs." The site is trying to sell its books, so watch out for sales pitches.

**Authority:** Petersons

## Weather and Climate (*see also* Earth Science; Geology; Physics)

### Cloud Guide

http://www.uen.org/utahlink/weather/clouds/cloud_id.html

This is a simple site with great photographs of clouds. It is a picture index to cloud types including: Altocumulus, Altostratus, Cirrocumulus, Cirrostratus, Cirrus, Cumulonimbus, Cumulus, Nimbostratus, Stratocumulus and Stratus. Links to other weather and cloud related sites are also available. (Grades K–8)

**Authority:** Unknown, KSL-TV has provided the photographs

### Franklin's Forecast

http://sln.fi.edu/weather/

Franklin's Forecast includes informative articles, curriculum connections, experiments, current weather resources and related website links. Topics range from lightning to El Niño. (Grades 4–9)

**Authority:** Franklin Institute Science Museum

### Hurricane and Tropical Storm Tracking

http://hurricane.terrapin.com/

Both Atlantic and Pacific Ocean storms are tracked, plotted and watched on this site. Information on hurricanes since 1886 is available. The site is updated via the GOES-8 east satellite and the GOES-9 west satellite.

**Authority:** Paul Curtis and Terrapin Associates

### Interactive Weather Information Network

http://iwin.nws.noaa.gov/iwin/graphicsversion/bigmain.html

This cool, graphics-intensive site gives current weather conditions for the United States. Live images of storm systems and temperatures are refreshed every five minutes. Active weather warnings for floods, severe thunderstorms, droughts, hurricanes, tornados and winter storms are available. A link to local weather brings up a clickable map. Choose a state to access state forecasts, zone forecasts, climatic data, watches and other data. Click on a region or city on the state map to get the current weather conditions. The main site contains a selection of videos about weather, a list of related links and a button for world weather.

**Authority:** U.S. National Weather Service

### Lightning and Atmospheric Electricity

http://thunder.msfc.nasa.gov/

The site includes a Lightning Primer which explains in great detail the history, characteristics, types, investigations, detections, studies and mapping of lightning. This primer is fully illustrated and includes references. (Grades 6–High School)

**Authority:** Steven J. Goodman, Ph.D., Will Ellett, Curator, NASA

### National Snow and Ice Data Center

http://www.nsidc.org/

The education resources section of this site is a list of links that have been selected for accuracy and quality. They include topics such as: Snow on the Web, Blizzards of 1996 and "Have Snow Shovel, Will

Travel." The main part of this site is a catalog of scientific data sets for the study of snow and ice.

**Authority:** U.S. National Oceans and Atmospheric Administration

## National Weather Service

http://www.nws.noaa.gov/

The mission statement of this site reads "The National Weather Service (NWS) provides weather, hydrologic and climate forecasts and warnings for the United States, its territories, adjacent waters and ocean areas, for the protection of life and property and the enhancement of the national economy." Information on this site is divided into several areas including: National, Regional, International and Specialized Centers. These areas include links to other websites or pages within this site. The map on the first page is clickable. It goes to a larger map from which you can click to get maps for specific areas and receive current site specific weather observations.

**Authority:** U.S. National Weather Service

## Online Guides to Meteorology

http://ww2010.atmos.uiuc.edu/(Gh)/guides/mtr/home.rxml

The Online Guide "is a collection of multimedia instructional modules that introduce and explain fundamental concepts in meteorology." Included are topics such as clouds, storms, El Niño, wind and atmospheric pressure. A detailed index of the site contents is available. (Grades 8–Undergraduate) ✎

**Authority:** Steve Hall, CoVis Project Coordinator, University of Illinois, Urbana-Champaign

## The Weather Channel's Storm Encyclopedia

http://www.weather.com/encyclopedia/

"This is the place that can answer your questions on severe and extreme weather. Here we cover the basics and some of the notable examples of Mother Nature's handiwork." Lists of weather information categories are provided, including: Flooding, Severe Thunderstorms, Heat Wave, Tornadoes, Hurricanes and Tropical Systems and Winter Storms. Click on one of these subjects to access the related articles. (Grades 6–Undergraduate)

**Authority:** The Weather Channel

## The Weather Unit

http://faldo.atmos.uiuc.edu/WEATHER/weather.html

A great place to find ideas and lesson plans for teaching weather. This site has been designed for elementary school-level education. There are lesson plans about weather using the following subjects: Math, Science,

Reading & Writing, Social Studies, Geography, Art, Music, Drama, Physical Education, Field Trips, Classroom Props, Resources and Other. (Grades K–6) ✎

**Authority:** Unknown

## WeatherNet

http://cirrus.sprl.umich.edu/wxnet/

This straightforward site states that it provides "access to thousands of forecasts, images and the Net's largest collection of weather links." Look for information via the subject categories or search for local weather by entering a city, state, country or zip code in the search box. ∞

**Authority:** Weather Underground, University of Michigan

# WebQuest (*see also* Education: Teacher and Student Resources)

## Jackie Carrigan's Webquest Collection

http://www.plainfield.k12.in.us/hschool/webquest.htm

This is a directory of WebQuests on the net. It can be browsed either by subject or by grade level. (Grades K–Undergraduate) ∞

**Authority:** Jackie Carrigan

## Kathy Schrock's Guide: WebQuest

http://school.discovery.com/schrockguide/webquest/webquest.html

Kathy Schrock has put together a great guide to WebQuests. The guide includes a Powerpoint file explaining what WebQuests are, a template and articles.

**Authority:** Kathy Schrock

## List of WebQuests

http://sesd.sk.ca/teacherresource/webquest/webquest.htm

More than 1,200 WebQuests are listed in this subject directory. The majority of the quests are for Science with Social Studies coming in a close second. There are WebQuests listed for art, business, technology, math, languages, drama and more.

**Authority:** Peter Arthur, SESD Teacher Resource Site

## WebQuest Page

http://edweb.sdsu.edu/webquest/webquest.html

Bernie Dodge is the creator of the WebQuest teaching model. "This site is designed to serve as a resource to those who are using the WebQuest model to teach with the Web. By pointing to excellent examples and collecting materials developed to communicate the idea, all of us experimenting with WebQuests will be able to learn from each other." The site is divided into several sections including Training Materials, What's New, Examples and Community. Both the site and the database of examples are searchable. There is a WebQuest webring located at the bottom of the page to help you find more WebQuest sites. A related page of WebQuest collections can be found at: http://edweb.sdsu.edu/webquest/webquest_collections.htm

**Authority:** Bernie Dodge, Educational Technology Dept., San Diego State University

# Women's Studies and Resources (*see also* Biography; History)

### Directory of Women's Organizations

http://electrapages.com/

Over 9,000 feminist groups are indexed on this page. You can search the directory by location, category, category & location or name. The button "Tour the Women's Movement" on the left button bar goes to a recommended list of links. ∞

**Authority:** Women's Information Exchange

### WIC: Women's Resources on the NET

http://www.wic.org/misc/resource.htm

The Women's International Center (WIC) sponsors this page of links. Their mission is to "Acknowledge, Honor and Encourage Women." The links do seem to be grouped by subject, but no subject headings are given. It is a quality list with links such as Amnesty International, Women in World History Curriculum, Notable Women Ancestors, Women's Business Network and the Hypatia Trust. ∞

**Authority:** Women's International Center

### Women's Studies Database

http://www.inform.umd.edu/EdRes/Topic/WomensStudies/

"The University of Maryland women's studies database, begun in September 1992, serves those people interested in the women's studies profession and in general women's issues." Both full-text resources and links to other websites are combined on this site. The contents are arranged into the following sections: Conferences, Announcements, Bibliographies, Calls for Papers, Computing, Employment, Government & History, Syllabi, Film Reviews, Gender Issues, Other

Websites, Program Support, Reading Room and Reference Room. The site is searchable.

**Authority:** Women's Studies Dept., University of Maryland

### WWWomen.com

http://www.wwwomen.com/

This site is a directory to similar in organizational style to Yahoo! To access the index, scroll down the page to the subject listings or use the keyword search box at the top of the page. Every website in the database is screened "for relevancy to women's interests." Subject categories include Women's Resources, Computers/Internet, Women in Business and Feminism. ∞

**Authority:** WWWomen, Inc.

# Zip and Postal Codes

### Postal Code Lookup

http://www.canadapost.ca/personal/tools/pcl/bin/default-e.asp

Canada Post produces this easy-to-use site. It is searchable by address, city or province.

**Authority:** Canada Post

### United States Postal Service Zip Codes

http://www.usps.gov/ncsc/ziplookup/lookupmenu.htm

The official Web page for accessing the government zip code database. It is searchable by address, city, state or zip code.

**Authority:** United States Postal Service

### Zip Codes & Country Codes of the World

http://www.escapeartist.com/global10/zip.htm

A centralized searchable database of international zip/postal code services on the Web. ∞

**Authority:** EscapeArtist

# Zoology (*see also* Biology; Science)

### Animal Info: Rare, Threatened and Endangered Mammals

http://www.animalinfo.org/

This site is searchable by keyword and both scientific and common names. It is also browsable by using the Species Group Index, World's Rarest Mammals list or Country Index. Each entry contains "a general summary about the animal's biology, history and threats." ∞

**Authority:** Paul Massicot

## Animals

http://www.connectingstudents.com/themes/
animals.htm

This section of a larger site is dedicated to information about animals. Connecting Students' mission is to "assist teachers by locating and listing websites that are worthwhile for students to visit." The Animals section is divided into the following sections: Resources, Books, Lesson Plans, Handouts and Web Based Activities. (Grades K–12) ∞

**Authority:** Connecting Students

## Endangered Species

http://eelink.net/EndSpp/

Information about endangered and extinct species in the United States is organized by region or by group. Links to international endangered species organizations, facts, data, pictures, current events, news and information are available. A section on Education and Interactive Kid Stuff includes links to web pages specifically designed for kids. (Grades K–Undergraduate) ∞ ✎

**Authority:** EE-Link

## Endangered Species Program

http://endangered.fws.gov/

The U.S. Fish and Wildlife Service is "working to conserve and restore endangered and threatened species and the ecosystems upon which they depend." To further this goal this website provides information on species, laws, policies, contacts and more. Of particular interest to teachers is the Kid's Corner, where they provide activities and free teaching materials.

**Authority:** U.S. Fish and Wildlife Service

## Entomology on the World Wide Web

http://www.colostate.edu/Depts/Entomology/
links.html

Indexing all kinds of bug-related links, this page is organized into one long alphabetical list. The sites include information on: butterflies, insects, bugs, silk worms, bees, beetles, moths and pests. Within the links are pages of lesson plans, articles, data sets, pictures and journals. (Grades K–Undergraduate) ∞

**Authority:** Entomology Dept., Colorado State University

## Evolution and Behavior

http://ccp.uchicago.edu/~jyin/evolution.html

This terrific site is an organized collection of links to evolution and behavior websites. These links are organized into the following broad categories: FAQs, Topics, Gurus, Archive, Classroom, Masterpiece, Groups and Messageboard. Within these links are amazing sites such as the EvoTutor http://www.evotutor.org/. ∞

**Authority:** Jie Yin

## Internet Resource Guide for Zoology

http://www.biosis.org/zrdocs/zoolinfo/zoolinfo.htm

Produced by BIOSIS a leading provider of biological information, this site is a free "index and guide to internet resources in the zoological and other related life sciences of interest to zoologists." Resources are grouped under subject headings such as invertebrates, helminths, arthropods, insects, chordates and vertebrates. It is searchable by keyword. ∞

**Authority:** BIOSIS and the Zoological Society of London

## Netfrog: Interactive Frog Dissection

http://curry.edschool.Virginia.EDU/go/frog/

This graphic site was originally designed for high school students. It includes a step-by-step dissection of a frog using Quicktime movies, pictures and text. (High School)

**Authority:** Mable Kinzie

# Zoology: Marine Biology (*see also* Biology; Science)

## Conchology

http://www.conchology.uunethost.be/

Everything you ever wanted to know about shells is contained or linked to this site. More than 50,000 scientific names and 4,000 images are available under the "cyber-conchology" section. Other sections include: available shells, collecting, links and collection management.

**Authority:** Guido T. Poppe

## Hardy's Internet Guide to Marine Gastropods

http://www.gastropods.com/

Easily the largest shell identification site on the Web. Hardy's Guide now indexes gastropods by both their scientific and common names, simplifying access. Most entries include pictures, books referenced and other identification data.

**Authority:** JZH Hardy

## Ichthyology Web Resources (IWR)

http://www.biology.ualberta.ca/jackson.hp/IWR/

IWR "compiles online ichthyology resources of scientific and educational value in an organized directory." Clickable sections are embedded in the explanatory text and include: Specimen Database, News, Content,

Taxon Pages, Ichthyology Community, Directory of Ichthyologists, Places and Museums. Within these sections are links to images, information, conferences, societies, news, articles and more. ∞

**Authority:** Keith L. Jackson

### MI-Net: Marine Institute's Navigatable Education Topics for K–12

http://www.mi.mun.ca/mi-net/topics.htm

There are 24 categories on this marine education site. They include topics such as Environment, Oceanography, Fisheries, Gallery and Ship Building. Entries include articles and information produced by the Marine Institute and links to outside resources. (Grades K–12) ∞

**Authority:** Marine Institute

### Oceanlink

http://oceanlink.island.net/

Both original content and linked resources are accessible on this site. The use of frames can confuse the viewer as to who is responsible for what content. However, there are tons of resources here including Ask a Marine Scientist, a question and answer forum and the Answer Archive, of more than 550 answers. Other popular sections include the OceanInfo a source for articles, a Glossary and Links. The site does not include a search engine.

**Authority:** Anne Stewart, OceanLink

# Zoology: Ornithology (see also
Biology; Science)

### Bird On!

http://birdcare.com/birdon/

All things avian can be found on this page, from bird news to bird care. The section titled Bird Book includes brief sketches of various species, a developing collection of in-depth portraits of particular species and an album of paintings and photographs by leading wildlife artists. The complete text of Peter Weaver's *Encyclopedia of Birdcare* and the *Birdwatcher's Dictionary* are also located on this site with additions being made by Chris Mead, Jacobi Jayne & Company.

**Authority:** Jacobi Jayne & Co.

### Bird Links to the World

http://www.bsc-eoc.org/links/

More than 8,000 bird-related links are indexed on this site. My favorite section is the Bird Webcam with links to cameras around the world that watch birds. Use the image map of the world to click to regional bird information. Alternately use the search box, the drop down menus or scroll down the page to view Lepage's "best bird websites."

**Authority:** Denis Lepage

### BirdSource: Birding with a Purpose

http://birdsource.cornell.edu/index.html

"BirdSource, a partnership of The Cornell Lab of Ornithology and the National Audubon Society offers insight into the dynamics of North American Bird populations with projects that track migration, irruption and foraging behavior." Bird enthusiasts are encouraged to share their records with BirdSource and to participate collecting date for the projects.

**Authority:** National Audubon Society and Cornell Lab of Ornithology

# Glossary

**boolean logic:** The use of "AND", "OR" and "NOT" in search statements. "AND" connects two or more concepts. "OR" increases synonym retrieval. "NOT" excludes specific concepts.

**browser:** A program which allows a computer to read hypertext documents and access the World Wide Web. Netscape Navigator, Microsoft's Internet Explorer, Opera and Lynx are examples of browsers.

**dialog box:** A small screen which pops up and allows the entry of information such as which drive to save to and what file name to save as. When the information has all been entered press "cancel," "save" or "ok," and the screen will go away.

**domain:** The last two- or three-letter code of a URL. .com, .gov, .au, .net, .edu are all domain designations. Two more were added in 2001: .biz and .info.

**drop down menu:** A small list of options available to use, such as "save," "copy," "paste," "file" and "new folder."

**e-mail:** The exchange of messages between individuals via the Internet.

**emoticons:** Smiley faces and other symbols that denote emotional states of mind. Frequently used in e-mail and Usenet discussions.

**FAQ:** Frequently Asked Questions, a list of answers to questions that are commonly posed about a specific topic. FAQs are generated by Usenet groups, mailing lists and by individual websites.

**FTP:** File Transfer Protocol, a program, now part of most web browsers, which allows a user on one computer to transfer files to and from another computer across the Internet.

**gopher:** A menu-driven, text-based system of documents and information sites that are accessible through most web browsers. This system has been largely superceded by the World Wide Web.

**home page:** The top-level document relating to an individual or institutional website. Sometimes home page is used generically and refers to any single web page.

**HTML:** Hypertext Markup Language, the language used to create web documents and sites. Codes are embedded in the document along with text which tell the browser how the document is supposed to look, which sites or pages it links to and which graphics, sound or animations to include. The word, Hypertext, is frequently substituted for the phrase, Hypertext Markup Language.

**HTTP:** Hypertext Transfer Protocol, the protocol that allows servers on the World Wide Web to interact.

**image map:** Active hypertext links that are part of a graphic. When the cursor is over any part of an active html link it will turn into a hand.

**Internet:** A global network that can be accessed via the World Wide Web, e-mail, FTP, telnet, or Usenet servers.

**link:** A word or image that is part of a web page which connects to another web page. Clicking on a link will bring up the other page on a web browser.

**log on/in:** The process of accessing or gaining entry to computer systems.

**log off:** The process of getting off a computer system.

**mailing lists:** A system of discussion groups that operate via e-mail. Majordomo and Listserv are common computer programs that run mailing lists. E-mail is sent to the central computer and then distributed to everyone who is subscribed to the mailing list.

**menu bar:** A list of items across the top of a software screen. The menu bar usually includes "File" and "Edit" along with other option that manipulate or use the software program.

**meta site:** A World Wide Website that indexes pages on the Internet that relate to a specific topic or subject. The site rarely creates new content, but provides access to existing web content.

**meta tag:** An HTML code that is invisible on a web page. Search engines use meta-tags to determine search relevancy. The most common meta-tags are description, keywords and author.

**modem:** A piece of hardware that can be installed in a computer or be used as an external add-on. It is used to dial-up servers and other computers.

**plug-in:** A software program that is loaded on a computer that is used in tandem with a web browser to display or play World Wide Web content.

**pop up window:** A small program window that overlays the original program and offers information, program options or a dialog box.

**server:** A computer that is a functional part of a network.

**telnet:** A computer program, now part of most web browsers, which allows a user to log on and use a remote computer's applications as if it were directly connected. This is frequently used for accessing library catalogs.

**Usenet:** An hierarchically arranged set of publicly available discussion forums. Usenet is frequently referred to as newsgroups.

**URL:** Uniform Resource Locator, is an Internet addressing system. Every document or site on the web has a distinctive URL.

**Web page:** Any single page on the World Wide Web.

**website:** A group of web pages that are produced by an individual or institution.

**World Wide Web:** A system of web server computers which host websites and documents. These computers are directly connected to the Internet. The websites link to each other via HyperText Markup Language (HTML). The World Wide Web is also known as the Web or the WWW.

# Website Title Index

# Subject Index

Websites are arranged in subject categories. The main subject categories used to organize the *Quick Guide* are bolded in this index. Sites with a strong subject focus in a subcategory have been given additional subject terms.